Ayoub Kafyulilo

Practical Use of ICT in Science and Mathematics Teachers' Training at DUCE

An Analysis of Prospective Teachers' Technological Pedagogical Content Knowledge

GRIN Publishing

Bibliographic information published by the German National Library:

The German National Library lists this publication in the National Bibliography; detailed bibliographic data are available on the Internet at http://dnb.dnb.de .

Imprint:

Copyright © 2011 GRIN Verlag GmbH
Print and binding: Books on Demand GmbH, Norderstedt Germany
ISBN: 978-3-656-02078-3

MSc Programme in Educational Science & Technology
Curriculum Instruction & Media Application

UNIVERSITEIT TWENTE.

Practical Use of ICT in Science and Mathematics Teachers' Training at Dar es Salaam University College of Education: An Analysis of Prospective Teachers' Technological Pedagogical Content Knowledge

Ayoub C Kafyulilo

Master's Thesis

University of Twente
Faculty of Behavioural Science
Educational Science and Technology
Curriculum Instruction and Media Application
Enschede, Netherlands

August 2010

Acknowledgement

Many people made significant contributions to successful completion of this study. I appreciate all materials and ideas incurred during the study by people who showed concern, love and care. Unfortunately, it is difficult to mention all of them individually but there are some whose immense contributions deserve special appreciations. I would like to express special gratitude and appreciations to Dr. Petra Fisser, Principal Supervisor of this study. She worked tirelessly in making constructive criticisms, ideas, and corrections from research proposal development to final report write-up. Her intellectual skills, comments, advice, commitments and close supervision are quite remarkable towards successful completion of my study. I also acknowledge the contribution of Dr. Joke Voogt, the Second Supervisor of this study, who continuously made a follow up of my progress and provided constructive advices for successful completion of this study.

I am very grateful to third year B.Ed Science students (2010) and their instructors from Dar es salaam University College of Education (DUCE) who heartedly accepted to participate in this study. They both provided constructive and useful information which helped me to gather the required information for the study. Their commitment, willingness and harmony during the study, are highly appreciated. I confer special thanks to Edward Winston who was always there to support me technically and materially. Together with Edward, I recognize the contribution of Onditi, H. Z., Nzilano, J., Mwalongo, A. and Kalinga, J. who accepted to be part of this study. In addition, I convey my special gratitude to Dr. J. Katabaro and Dr. F. Mafumiko who always showed concern to my academic development.

I would like also to express a heartfelt appreciation to all people who in one way or another supported my nomination in the University of Twente Scholarships. Their decision has been of substantial impact to my life, my institution and my country. I would also like to give special thanks to Jan Nelissen and Monique Davids for their outstanding effort to ensure that my life at the University of Twente is as smooth as possible. I appreciate the motivation and support I got from Kassim Nihuka, Carolin Richtering and Yonas Yosef in the process of preparing my final report. I adore the company I got from Efraim Kosia (Tanzania), Zenebe Hailesellassie (Ethiopia), Wilson Chilembo (Zambia), Larissa Odendaal and Rinse Jelluma (Netherlands) who were always ready to share their experience and knowledge in different aspects of research. Lastly, I am grateful to DUCE management, for giving me a permission to attend studies on the Master of Science in Educational Science and Technology.

Ayoub C Kafyulilo
Enschede, Netherlands

Table of Contents

List of Tables

List of Acronyms

CK	Content Knowledge
Connect-TED	Connect - Teacher Education Development
DUCE	Dar es salaam University College of Education
ICT	Information and Communication Technology
ICT_TPD	Information and Communication Technology for Teacher Professional Development
ISTE	International Society for Science in Education
TK	Technological Knowledge
PCK	Pedagogical Content Knowledge
PK	Pedagogical Knowledge
TCK	Technological Content Knowledge
TPK	Technological Pedagogical Knowledge
TPACK	Technological Pedagogical Content Knowledge
UNESCO	United Nations Educational Scientific and Cultural Organization
URT	United Republic of Tanzania

Abstract

This study investigated the ways through which pre-service science and mathematics teachers at Dar es Salaam University College of Education (DUCE) can acquire competencies for integrating technology pedagogy and content in teaching. Specifically the study investigated the preservice teachers' ICT integration competencies; practices that can be effective in enhancing pre-service science and mathematics teachers' competency in integrating technology, pedagogy and content; as well as the impact of those practices in the development of preservice teachers' technological pedagogical content knowledge. An action research approach was employed in the study, employing the pre and post-intervention assessment of preservice teachers' knowledge on technology, pedagogy and content. Planed interventions were carried out during the study, to enable preservice teachers to identify areas of weaknesses in their technology integration competencies, and propose alternative approaches for addressing the identified weaknesses. Student questionnaire, instructor interview and observation checklist were used to collect date before, during and after intervention. Researcher's log book, digital camera and audio recorder were used in recording events and activities taking place during the study. Findings revealed that when preservice teachers engage in hands on activities such as microteaching, lesson design and the opportunity to share their ideas with peers, they easily developed their technological pedagogical content knowledge. An analysis of knowledge change after the intervention, showed a significant difference between pre-intervention and post intervention preservice teachers' knowledge of TPACK. It is therefore concluded that, the adoption of hands on activities that uses technology and involve teachers in planning of what to teach, how to teach and with what technology to teach, and provision of an opportunity to share this plan with colleagues, can make a significant change in the development of TPACK among preservice teachers.

Chapter One

Background of the Study

1.1 Introduction

Teaching and Learning in science and mathematics place a lot of challenges to teachers and is setting an alarm to stakeholders in education: government, parents and schools. Many countries are currently experiencing a gradual dropdown on students' participation and performance in science and mathematics subjects (Beauchamp & Parkinson, 2008; Ezeife, 2003; Martin et al, 2008; Mwinshekke, 2003). Failure in these subjects is raising a debate on how teachers teach and how students learn. Some see the failure as being born from teachers due to lack of important teaching competencies, while others see the failure as resulting from lack of students motivation in science and mathematics (Yunus, & Ali, 2009). However, Koehler & Mishra (2009) see the problem as being caused by both teaching approaches and the way students learn. Thus, they call for an approach that treats teaching as an interaction between what teachers know and how they apply what they know in the unique circumstance or contexts within their classroom. Luis, Illera & Escofet (2009), support the idea of Kohler & Mishra, by proposing the adoption of learner centered approach, an approach which is widely promoted throughout the world for its impact in students' learning. However, effective learner centered approach requires the use of Information and Communication Technologies (ICT) which engage students in a flexible learning that allows dynamism in terms of location, time, materials, content and teaching approaches (Collis & Moonen, 2001).

Thus this study proposed the integration of ICT in science and mathematics teaching and learning. ICT has been referred as all products that can store, retrieve, manipulate, transmit or receive information electronically in a digital form, for example: personal computers, television, digital camera and other electronic hardware and software tools (Luppicini, 2005). Studies (Tilya, 2008; Senzige & Sarukesi, 2003; Voogt, 2003) have shown that use of ICT in teaching has a lot of advantages to teachers and students. For example a study by Keong, Horani & Daniel (2005) revealed that ICT use improves the way science and mathematics is taught and enhances students' understanding of basic concepts of science and mathematics (cf. Voogt, 2003). Studies done by Niess et al. (2009), Beauchamp & Parkinson (2008) and Senzige & Sarukesi (2003) are currently addressing the importance of incorporating ICT in science and mathematics teaching, to overcome the existing failures in those subjects. The use of ICT in teaching, presents a paradigm shift from a teacher centered to a learner-centered, from individual learning to collaborative learning, and from a teacher as a source of knowledge to a learner as source of knowledge (Collis & Moonen, 2001; Nieveen, Handelzalts, van den Akker & Homminga, 2005). The ability to harness ICT in the design of the classrooms learning can have an impact in the engagement of students in the learning of science and mathematics, by creating more options for learners to connect technology with course content (cf. Dominique & Fereirra, 2008).

Despite the importance that ICT integration in education has in enhancing teaching and learning in science and mathematics (Niess et al, 2009; Voogt, 2003), less has been done to integrate it in education in developing countries. Most developing countries are currently developing ICT policies (Hare, 2007; Moonen, 2008; Tilya, 2008) which in most educational practices, their impacts are found to be insignificant (Ottevanger, Van den Akker & Feiter, 2007). These policies are reported to place a great deal of emphasis on providing ICT infrastructure to secondary and primary schools Gaible & Burns (2005) rather than their use in teaching (Unwin, 2005). For example, in Tanzania, ICT use is found to be limited to teaching basic ICT skills, and not integrated as a medium of instruction (Ottevanger et al, 2007). Also Tilya (2008) and Sugiyama (2005) reported that, majority of teachers in Tanzania are not using ICT in their teaching. The poor ICT uptake by teachers in schools is reported to result from lack of teachers' motivation and self confidence (Cox, Preston & Cox, 1999; Pelgrrum, 2001), which is caused by lack of technological knowledge (VanFossen, 1999) and the fear that ICT is complicated and difficult to use

1

(Snoeyink & Ertmer, 2001). Additionally, there are some teachers who are reluctant to change their traditional pedagogical practices (Snoeyink & Ertmer, 2001), and some of them believe that technology does not enhance learning (Yuen & Ma, 2002).

The inappropriate integration of technology in teaching is raising doubts as to whether teachers are disinterested to use technology or they were not well trained to integrate technology in teaching. This, calls for an investigation of the teacher training program to find out the way teachers are taught to work with technology. Unlike other professions, teacher training programs are expected to develop basic technological skills, operational skills and professionalism skills (ISTE, 2008). The development of skills in these three components is expected to foster the development of teachers' knowledge, skills and ability to integrate technology into their teaching. This will consequently cultivate the development of technological pedagogical and content knowledge and the manner in which they (technology, pedagogy and content) are integrated.

According to Koehler &Mishra (2009), "at the heart of good teaching with technology are three core components: content, pedagogy, and technology, plus the relationships among and between them" (p.62). A teacher needs to have these three knowledge bases (content, pedagogy, and technology) which form the core of the technological pedagogical content knowledge (TPACK) framework. TPACK is the promising framework for preparation of teachers who can integrate technology in their teaching. Thus, teachers' training colleges are argued to focus on how they develop preservice teachers' knowledge of using technology in relation to pedagogy and content, which makes up the TPACK. TPACK is the basis of good teaching with technology and requires an understanding of the representation of concepts using technologies". Doering, Hughes & Hoffman (2003), argue that in most cases, teachers preparation program have been the problem in developing preservice teachers who are competent in technology integration. Thus, a study to investigate what can be done at the teacher training college, how can it be done and what will be the impact was found to be important, thus a reason for conducting this study at DUCE.

1.2 Statement of the Problem

Knowledge of technology, pedagogy and content is important to preservice teachers for effective integration of technologies in science and mathematics teaching. Teacher training institutions as gateways to effective teaching with technology are required to develop these ICT integration competencies to preservice teachers. Although there are evidences from the courses offered in colleges, that preservice teachers are taught on how to use ICT in teaching science and mathematics, studies (Hare, 2007; Kafanabo, 2006; Sugiyama, 2005; Tilya, 2008) have reported a low level of ICT uptake in schools in Tanzania. Studies have further reported that, the extent to which teachers will integrate technology in teaching depends largely on the way they learned with technology (Doering et al, 2003; LeBaron, McDonough & Robinson, 2008). The later statement suggests that, the poor uptake of technology in teaching is the outcome of the poor training that teachers get from colleges. However, there is no evidence yet to prove that preservice teachers are not well trained to integrate technology in teaching. Most of the studies carried out in Tanzania on ICT integration in teaching, paid great attention on the teachers' use of ICT in teaching at school rather than how a teacher is prepare to use ICT. This makes it difficult to explain the way preservice teachers are trained to integrate technology, pedagogy and content in teaching. Thus this study was determined to investigate the competencies that preservice teachers develop from the college on ICT integration in teaching, effective practices that can enhance preservice teachers' ability to integrate technology, pedagogy and content and the impacts of those practices in developing preservice teachers' technological pedagogical content knowledge.

2

1.3 Research Questions

The problem stated above leads to the main research question which is formulated as: *"How can science and mathematics preservice teachers acquire competencies for integrating technology, pedagogy and content in their teaching?"* This main research question was answered by dividing the question into several sub questions:

The first sub question is related to ICT integration competencies that preservice teachers have already acquired from DUCE, and is formulated as: "What competencies do pre-service science and mathematics teachers at DUCE have, in relation to the use of ICT in teaching?"

The second question is about practices (interventions activities) that have potential impact in the development of preservice teachers' competency in integrating technology with pedagogy and content and is formulated as: "What practices are effective in promoting the preservice teachers' competencies in integrating technology with content and pedagogy at DUCE?"

The third question is related to the outcomes of the intervention activities carried out in question two and is formulated as: "What are the impacts of intervention activities in developing pre-service science and mathematics teachers' technological pedagogical content knowledge (TPACK)?"

1.4 Contribution of the Study

This study was determined to investigate the relationship existing between what teachers learn from the teachers training college and what teachers practice in the teaching field. Through this study, it can be established whether the low uptake of ICT by teachers in science and mathematics teaching, is resulting from teachers themselves or the manner in which they are taught to integrate technology in their teaching. During the study, preservice teachers at DUCE engaged in different hands on activities, such as microteaching, TPACK training, lesson design, lesson presentation and discussion with peers. Participation in these intervention activities was important in the development of an understanding of the preservice teachers on how technology pedagogy and content can be integrated in the teaching process. These interventions activities can therefore enhance preservice teachers' ability to integrate technology in their teaching. Also the interventions can be adopted by college instructors as a new approach for enhancing learning of technology integration, by involving preservice teachers in a number of hands on activities. In addition, participants in the study will become ambassadors of TPACK to all other teachers in schools where they will be employed to work. As they integrate technology in their teaching, they may become models to other teachers who may also be interested to adopt their teaching approaches.

1.5 Overview of the Study

This study is organized into six chapters; where as the first chapter presented an overall introduction to the study, the statement of the problem and research questions. The description of the context in which the study was carried out is covered in Chapter two. The chapter discusses the ICT policy in education in Tanzania, ICT in schools and teachers training colleges as well as ICT implementation in schools. Chapter three presents the review of literature related to technology integration in education and the overall conception of TPACK. In the literature review a comprehensive analysis of previous studies on the concept of TPACK and its use in the preservice science and mathematics teachers' preparation has been covered. In chapter four, a research design has been described, presenting the participants, instruments and data collection procedures. Chapter five provides the findings of the study. Findings are organized according to the research questions that the study intended to answer. The last part of this study is chapter six which presents the summary of the findings, discussion, conclusion and recommendations.

3

Chapter Two

The Context of Tanzania

This chapter describes the overall teaching and learning in science and mathematics in Tanzania and the extent to which ICT is integrated in teaching. The chapter is organized into six sections; where as, section 2.1 describes the teaching and learning in science and mathematics in secondary schools. Section 2.2 discusses the ICT policy in Tanzania and section 2.3 describes the ICT use in schools. ICT integration in teacher training colleges has been discussed in section 2.4 where as ICT integration situation at DUCE has been presented in section 2.5. The hindering and promoting factors for implementation of ICT in education in Tanzania have been discussed in section 2.6.

2.1 Teaching and Learning in Science and Mathematics

Teaching and learning in science and mathematics subjects has for a long time been a challenge in Tanzania secondary and primary schools. Since 1970s there has been an alarming decline in the level of participation and performance in science and mathematics in both primary and secondary schools in Tanzania (Mwinsheikke, 2003). The failure rates in mathematics in secondary schools, from 1995 to 2002 reached 70% (Sugiyama, 2005). A report by the Mathematical Association of Tanzania (MAT) shows that from 2003 to 2007 the failure rates in Basic Mathematics reached 73% (United Republic of Tanzania [URT], 2008). According to the National Examination Council of Tanzania Examination Cycle for 2002-2008, failure rates in physics and biology from 2002 to 2007 were between 40-46% in physics and between 45-76% in biology. Studies (Kitta, 2004; Sugiyama, 2005) show that, majority of students participating in science (physics, chemistry, and biology) and mathematics subjects, at their secondary education levels do fail. While the country is in great demand of engineers, doctors, accountants, science and mathematics teachers as well as agricultural officers, the number of students engaging in science is decreasing year after year. When addressing the parliament meeting on 29th August 2008, Hon. Mizengo Pinda, the Prime Minister of Tanzania, described the failures in science and mathematics as undermining country's efforts for development in science and technology (URT, 2008).

Poor performance in science and mathematics has been attributed to among many factors, the absence of competent teachers, lack of science teaching and learning resources as well as shortage of science and mathematics teachers in most schools (URT, 2008). In acknowledging the fact that teachers are the sole source for educational change and improvement of students' learning, the government of Tanzania has since 1960s taken several initiatives to enhance teaching, learning and performance in Science and Mathematics. The first initiative was the establishment of a Mathematics Association of Tanzania (MAT) in 1966, which aimed at uniting Mathematics teachers in the country so that they can exchange experiences and techniques of teaching Mathematics (http://maths.udsm.ac.tz/mat/index.htm). However, since its establishment there has been no improvement of students learning outcomes in mathematics, rather a gradual drop down has been observed (O-saki, 2007; Sugiyama, 2005, Kitta, 2004).

From 1990s, the government of Tanzania in collaboration with different international organizations introduced several projects which intended at enhancing science and mathematics teaching approaches, preparing new teaching resources including books and training more science and mathematics teachers. Example of projects carried out includes;

1. The Science Education in Secondary Schools (SESS) Project, funded by GTZ-German in 1997, which aimed at improving the teaching and learning of science and mathematics in secondary schools (O-level) in Tanzania. It concentrated on in-service teacher education and training of resource persons (O-saki, 2007);

2. The Teacher Education in Mathematics and Science (TEAMS) from 1996 to 2004, funded by Dutch government, focusing on review of undergraduate science teacher education programs at the University of Dar es Salaam and developing in-service training materials (cf. Ottevanger, Faiter, O-saki & van den Akker, 2005);

Despite all those initiatives taken by the government of Tanzania to overcome the massive failure of students in science and mathematics, the situation has remained hectic year after year (O-saki, 2007). ICT integration in science and mathematics teaching remains to be the only promising method to enhance learning in these subjects (Keong et al, 2005). In a research by Keong et al. (2005) and Voogt (2003) it was revealed that, use of ICT in teaching science and mathematics improves learning through increased collaboration among students through the increased level of communication and sharing of knowledge. It was also found that ICT helps teachers to provide a rapid and accurate feedback to students and allow students to focus on strategies and interpretations of answers rather than spending time on tedious computational calculations. Keong and colleagues also report that constructivist pedagogical approach is easily supported by ICT (cf. Tilya, 2003; Voogt, 2003), where students use technology to explore and reach an understanding of mathematical concepts by concentrating on problems solving process rather than on calculations related to the problems. Thus, ICT integration in science and mathematics teaching and learning can be a promising solution to the long existed students' failure in science and mathematics in Tanzania.

2.2 ICT Policy in Tanzania

The development and growth of technology integration in education in Tanzania started as early as 1980s, when the science and technology policy of Tanzania was formulated. This was followed by the formation of Tanzania Commission for Science and Technology (COSTECH) in 1986 and the formation of the Ministry of Science, Technology and Higher Education (MSTHE) in 1990 (Mambo, 2001). Since 1990s, Tanzania established a good number of training institutions which intended to promote research and development in science, technology and education. However, the government of Tanzania was not able to sustain those institutions financially; this made them academically unviable. Failure of ICT to produce the desired results in most of the fields including education in the early 1990s was caused by the lack of a policy on information technology, its acquisition and use.

The first national ICT policy in Tanzania was developed in 2003 (URT, 2003). This policy had two main objectives: first, was to provide a national framework to enable ICT to contribute towards achieving national development goals; and the second was to transform Tanzania into a knowledge-based society through the application of ICT. Although the 2003 policy mentioned education as one of the areas of its focus, still the policy was too vague and thus could not address specific components of ICT integration in education. In 2007 the *ICT policy for basic education* was formulated which aimed to promote the acquisition and appropriate use of literary, social, scientific, vocational, technological, professional and other forms of knowledge, skills and understanding for the development and improvement of man and society (URT, 2007). This policy incorporates the integration of ICTs in pre-primary, primary, secondary and teacher education, as well as non-formal and adult education (Hare, 2007; URT, 2007).

The ICT policy for basic education considers issues of ICT infrastructure; curriculum and content; training and capacity development; planning procurement and administration. It also pays attention on the management, support and sustainability, and monitoring and evaluation (Hare, 2007; URT, 2007). The ICT policy for basic education is implemented in collaboration with other education policy documents which govern the education sector in Tanzania in general. These are the Education and Training Policy of 1995, the Primary Education and Development Plan (PEDP) 2002-2006, and the Secondary Education Development Plan (SEDP) 2004-2009 (URT, 2009). All three documents emphasize the need for access to and improved quality of education for all despite the increasing number of enrolments. Both PEDP and

SEDP prioritize ICT-based information management at all levels and an introduction of computer courses into primary and secondary education (Hare, 2007; URT, 2009).

2.3 ICT in Schools

The process to introduce ICT in education started as far back as 1997, when the first official syllabus for school computer studies was introduced (Mambo, 2001; Tilya, 2003; URT, 2003). Since 1997 little was done to have ICT integrated in education, until 2002 is when ICT integration initiatives started in education in Tanzania. It was in 2002 when a stakeholders' workshop was called by the ministry of education with support from the International Institute for Communications Development (IICD), a Dutch NGO (Hare, 2007). According to Hare, the workshop identified areas of ICT interventions and 11 project proposals were generated to raise awareness of the benefits and the potential gains in adopting ICT in the education sector. In 2005, the Ministry of Education and Vocation Training (MOEVT) formed an e-school forum to design a programme supporting the introduction and use of ICT for secondary education known as the "e-School Programme". The program aimed at introducing ICT in secondary schools, in phases starting with 200 schools in phase 1 (2006 to 2008), a large scale rollout covering 2,000 schools in phase 2 (in a five years period), and nationwide coverage by 2015. The project covers a wide range of activities including ICT infrastructure development in the schools, technical resources, student management at school levels, content and curriculum development, e-learning, sensitization, human resources development, and programme co-ordination and funding.

Although there have been initiatives for integrating ICT in education since 1997, a study by Vesisenaho in 2007, ten years later, shows that mostly private secondary schools in Tanzania are the one which are able to offer ICT integration in teaching. Vesisenaho's findings are supported by Hare (2007), who reports that; "mostly private schools in the urban centers, especially Dar es Salaam, are the one which are using ICTs, albeit without a formal setting or a policy framework" (p. 4) (cf. Ottevanger et al, 2007; Tilya, 2003). More over, these ICTs are mostly confined to administration purposes. There is some limited use for teaching basic ICT skills, and in most cases ICTs have not been integrated as a medium of instruction. Kafanabo (2006) and Tilya (2008) report that in schools where ICT is used, students are mostly taught on how to switch on and off the computer, as well as some basic computer program such as Microsoft Word, Excel and PowePoint. In areas where there is internet connection they also learn internet applications. Teachers are not yet using ICT as a tool to enhance teaching and learning in their subjects. The delay in the development of ICT integration in education is caused by the apparent lack of commitment and inadequate resources from the government for information technology, lack of competent teachers and delay of an effective information technology policy in education (Hare, 2007; Tilya, 2008). As a method of addressing incompetency in ICT integration in teaching among teachers, the Ministry of Education and Vocational Training (MoEVT) formulated the Information and Communication Technology for Teacher Professional Development (ICT-TPD) framework (URT, 2009). The framework was developed to address challenges of teacher shortages in key subjects (Mathematics and Science), teacher quality and teacher support using the existing ICT infrastructure in the Teacher Training Colleges (TTCs) for pre-service and in-service programmes and on-going learning of teachers (URT, 2009).

2.4 ICT in Teacher Training Colleges

2.4.1 General Situation

The Ministry of Education in Tanzania, through the support by the Swedish International Development Cooperation Agency (Sida), initiated the ICT-Connect-TED programme for introducing ICT in teachers' training colleges (TTC) in 2002. The programme was initiated on the view that, the poor performance of teachers in science and mathematics teaching is often caused by a lack of information and the absence of the means to communicate and cooperate effectively with their peers in other schools. Thus, the programme aimed at improving the quality of teacher education by using ICTs to improve both pre-service and in-service teacher education (Hare, 2007). ICT-Connect-TED has managed to provide 44 teachers training colleges in Tanzania with computers and networking infrastructure that allows participating teachers to exchange information through internet. By the end of 2004, the project had managed to achieve its goal of connecting all Tanzania's teacher training colleges with the internets and setting up a network that links all of them together. The project is now focusing on content development, via a regular newsletter and other communication related activities including ICT training for TTC staff (IICD, 2010). It is expected that at the end of ICT-Connect-TED project, all colleges will be equipped with thin client computers with a server and internet access. Tutor technicians are also being trained on support and networking essentials to be able to offer installation and maintenance services to colleges. Although TTCs were equipped with ICT facilities since 2004, the ICT integration competency of the preservice teachers graduating from these colleges is still low (Tilya, 2008). No researches have been done yet to investigate how preservice teachers are trained to integrate technology with pedagogy and content in their teaching. But there is a great likelihood that, the ICT facilities available in colleges are not appropriately used to train teachers to become competent users of ICT in teaching.

2.4.2 The Situation at DUCE

The Dar es Salaam University College of Education (DUCE) is among the two constituent colleges of the University of Dar es salaam (the other being Mkwawa University College of Education), which were established by the Government of Tanzania in September 2005 to address the problem of acute shortage of graduate teachers as a result of the expansion of primary education enrolment through the Primary Education Development Plan (PEDP) (2002- 2006) and the creation of new secondary schools through the Secondary Education Development Plan (SEDP) (2004 -2009). The two government initiatives (PEDP & SEDP) created an enhanced demand for graduate teachers and tutors in the country. Being one of the public higher education institutions, DUCE has its primary business of educating and training, carrying out research and providing public service for improved quality of life of the Tanzanian people. The college envisages of becoming a reputable higher institution that efficiently gives high quality services with diligence as its *vision* and it strives to provide integrated high quality teaching, research, and consultancy services as its *mission* (www.duce.ac.tz).

At the moment DUCE has a population of 3550 students enrolled in four degree programmes (Bachelor of Arts with Education (BA.Ed), Bachelor of Science with Education (B.Sc.Ed), Bachelor of Education in Arts (B.Ed Arts) and Bachelor of Education in Science (B.Ed. Science). These degree programs are offered by three faculties (Faculty of Humanities and Social Sciences, Faculty of Science and Faculty of Education. The total number of staff is about 310 where by 159 (53.3%) are academic members of staff. The Bachelor of Education in Science; one of the degree programs offered by DUCE enrolls students with different science (Physics, Chemistry and Biology) and mathematics backgrounds. One of the expected learning outcomes from this Bachelor program is to provide sufficient depth in an academic discipline (Mathematics, Physics, Chemistry and Biology), focusing on the development of concepts and ideas as well as basic requirements of the modern school curriculum. In addressing the need for teachers who fit in the modern society and modern school curriculum, DUCE offers three ICT related courses to pre-service science and mathematics teachers: Computer Literacy for Teachers (3 units), Educational Media and Technology (3 units), and ICT in Science and Mathematics Education (3 units). 1 unit is equivalent to 15 one hour lectures; thus, 3 units is equivalent to 15 two hour lectures and 15 one hour seminars thus, a total of 45 hours (http://www.udsm.ac.tz/undergraduate/DUCE2009-10.pdf). The three courses are expected to provide a wide range of experiences to preservice teachers on how to work with technology and are widely offered by most teacher training colleges in the country.

However, DUCE as it is for most teachers training institutions in the country is experiencing some challenges in offering ICT related course. One of the challenges is insufficient ICT infrastructure and a lack of technological knowledge among the college instructors. The college has two computer labs, one in the faculty of education with approximately 10 working computers and the other in the faculty of science with approximately 20 working computers. In total there are 30 computers for 3500 students. Similarly there is one computer for the college staffs in each department with about 15 members of staff. Thus, the computer to student ratio is 1:117 and computer to staff ratio is 1:15. Computer labs are mostly open when there is an ICT related class which requires the use of computer. There is also one laptop and one projector in each faculty with over 60 academic staffs. In addition the college has only one television set to facilitate students learning. Overall, the college gets a very low internet bandwidth which makes it difficult for most synchronous communication and access to some learning sites that requires high bandwidth such as YouTube. This situation is found to affect the ICT use among instructors and preservice teachers, thus raising questions on whether preservice teachers at DUCE acquire the required competencies for ICT integration in teaching or not.

2.5 Implementing ICT in Education in Tanzania: What Helps and What Hinders

Hare (2007) and Resta & Laferriere (2008), present several factors which can either promote or hinder the implementation of ICT in teaching and learning. Table 1 presents the hindering and promoting factors to ICT implementation in secondary schools in Tanzania.

Table 1: *Enabling and Constraining Factors for ICT Implementation in Schools (Hare, 2007)*

Factors	Enabling Features	Constraints Features
Policy framework and implementation	The new policy (ICT in basic Education of 2007), is expected to help in guiding the development of ICT in education and therefore make the ministry assume leadership	The policy puts emphasis on the installation of hardware in schools with less attention on the benefits teachers and students can get from ICT (Hare, 2007).
Infrastructure and cost of bandwidth	More hardware and software are being installed in colleges and secondary schools (cf. Resta & Laferriere, 2008)	Despite the liberalization of the telecommunications sector, the cost of bandwidth is still out of reach of many schools especially in rural areas.
Language of the Internet	Currently there are online content in Kiswahili and some applications come with Kiswahili dictionaries. The advent of open source software has helped localize ICTs and the Internet and thusincreased access	Language has been identified as one of the major inhibitors of ICT use in Tanzania. Many people are comfortable in Kiswahili and only learn English in later years of primary school or early secondary school.
Electricity		The national electricity grid is still limited to commercially viable areas missing out most of the schools, which are in the rural areas. This has increased the cost of owning ICT infrastructure.
Tutor technicians		ICT in education is still a new concept. The teachers- colleges are now training teachers in ICT. A lot more effort will be required to give in-service training to teachers in ICT.
New technologies	There is proliferation of new technologies that are promising to drastically lower the cost of entry and ownership of ICT in schools. These include open source software and wireless connectivity which have a wider coverage in the country.	Majority of teachers and student are not competent in using most of the new technological tools thus a need for training so as to be able to use those ICT tools (cf. Resta & Laferriere, 2008).

8

Resta & Laferriere (2008) also mention access to hardware, software, connectivity to the internet and access to high quality, culturally relevant content in local language as one of the challenges to effective integration of ICT in education. They also describe that access to creating, sharing and exchanging digital content and access to educators who know how to use digital tools and resources as other challenges. In addition, Resta & Laferriere put forward the importance of high quality research on the application of digital technologies to enhance learning. Absence of such researches hinders the understanding of the effective ICT integration approaches that can be of beneficial to students' learning. This is true for Tanzania, where there are limited studies on the integration of technology pedagogy and content, which are the core of good teaching with technology. Thus this study seems important in a way towards the integration between pedagogical content knowledge and technological knowledge which has for a long time missed in the researches carried out in Tanzania.

Chapter Three

Theoretical Framework

This chapter provides a summary of literature related to technology integration in education and TPACK framework. The review is presented in five sub-sections which includes; ICT integration in education (section 3.1), TPACK in science and mathematics teaching (section 3.2), TPACK Competencies for Pre-service Science and Mathematics Teachers (section 3.3) and TPACK training package for preservice teachers (section 3.4). It also provides a summary and way forward towards preservice teachers TPACK development in section 3.5.

3.1 ICT Integration in Education

The idea of integrated knowledge of teachers is not new in teacher education. Discussion about the interplay of different components of knowledge to enhance teaching competencies started as far back as 1980s. One of the pioneers of the integrated knowledge for teachers was Shulman (1986) who focused on the importance of treating pedagogy and content knowledge as basic requirement for teacher training. Shulman traced as far back as 1870s, when pedagogy was ignored and attention was paid on content, and further in 1980 when it was conspicuously absent. *"I propose that we look back even further than those 1875 tests for teachers and examine the history of the university as an institution to discern the sources for this distinction between content knowledge and pedagogical method"* (Shulman, 1986, 6). Since the presentation of the idea of pedagogical content knowledge (PCK) as a basis for teachers to deliver the required learning outcomes, there existed quietness until the early 1990s when the idea of technology started to be introduced in schools. In 1993, Marcinkiewicz, in his paper, "factors influencing computer use in the classroom", described how easily or difficult could computer technology be integrated in teaching (cf. Voogt, 1993). Marcinkiewicz focused his discussion on how the attitude of teachers towards computer use in teaching is important in having technology integrated in education. Also in 1998, the International Society for Technology in Education (ISTE) developed the so called National Educational Technology Standards for teachers and students. In 2000, Roblyer reviewed those standards and provided a description on how best technology can be integrated in teaching to offer pleasing learning outcomes.

Most of the studies done from 1990s to 2000 had more focus on the overall use of technology in education. These studies put less attention on the relationship between technology and the previously identified competencies for teachers on pedagogical content knowledge. In 2005 two publications were made on the integration of pedagogy, content and technology. Niess (2005) tried to make a link between pedagogical content knowledge based on Shulmans idea, and technological knowledge, and described how the three components can interact to form TPCK. Mishra & Koehler (2005) also came up with the idea of TPCK as a core of good teaching with technology being as well built on the idea of Shulman. However the difference between the concepts put forward by Mishra & Koeler and that proposed by Niess, is that while Mishra & Koehler consider technology as everything that can support learning (pencil, chalkboard, analogy and digital equipments), Niess discussed technology in reference to analogy and digital equipments alone. In addition, Mishra & Koehler (2005) discussed technology integration in the general education while Niess (2005) focused on a specific subject (Mathematics). But both had a common idea of developing teachers' knowledge on technology, pedagogy and content as important attributes for effective teaching with technology.

It is Mishra & Koehler (2006, 2009) who extended TPCK to TPACK and added the context as one of the important components in thinking of the integration between technology, pedagogy and content (cf. Harris, Mishra & Koehler, 2009). The context may refer to grade level of the students, schools or a class in which the technology is used. According to Koehler & Mishra (2009), teachers need to know what and how they apply technology in the unique contexts within their classrooms. A teacher is urged to also develop an ability to flexibly navigate the spaces defined by the three elements; content, pedagogy, and technology and the complex interactions among these elements in specific contexts (cf. Koehler & Mishra, 2009; Voogt, Tilya & van den Akker, 2009). Thus, technology integration programs should focus on the development of teachers' knowledge of integrating technology, pedagogy and content.

3.2 TPACK in Science and Mathematics Teaching

There is a growing body of research (Niess et al, 2009) which indicates that, technologies, including graphing, and some computer based mathematics learning programs can enhance students' conceptual and procedural knowledge of mathematics (Özgün-Koca, Meagher & Edwards, 2010; Webb, 2008). When teachers decide whether and how to use technology in their teaching, they need to consider the science or mathematics content that they will teach, the technology that they will use, and the pedagogical methods that they will employ" (Ozgun-Koca et al, 2010). This requires teachers to reflect on the critical relationships between content, technology and pedagogy (Koehler & Mishra, 2009; Niess et al, 2009). However, the ability of teachers to establish the relationship between content, pedagogy and technology, depends largely on the way they were taught to integrate technology in teaching. In the late 1980s and early 1990s, an examination of teachers' science and mathematics PCK, revealed an overarching conception that teachers' beliefs about how to teach science and mathematics generally were aligned with how they learned science and mathematics (Beyerbach et al, 2001; Niess et al, 2009). Teachers who learned to solve science and mathematics problems through the use of graphing calculators, spreadsheets and some learning software were among the few who embraced the use of those tools in teaching science and mathematics (Niess et al, 2009).

Niess and colleagues, see the low uptake of technology by teachers as being mostly associated with the poor knowledge of science and mathematics, instructional strategies and representations of a particular science or mathematical topics supported by digital technologies to demonstration, verification, and drill and practice (cf. Koehler & Mishra, 2009; Webb, 2008). Also their knowledge of students' understandings, thinking, and learning in mathematics held to the importance of mastery of skills with paper and pencil prior to using modern digital technologies was found to hinder the uptake of technology by teachers (Kastberg & Leatham, 2005, cited in Niess et al, 2009). In their study, Niess and colleagues found that, access to technology without necessary knowledge of related science and mathematics curriculum materials did not encourage teachers to incorporate the technology in their classroom instruction. Thus, a reason why Mishra & Koehler (2009) insist on the need for teachers to know, not only the subject matter they teach but also the manner in which the subject matter can be changed by the application of technology. Thus, the need for science and mathematics teachers to participate in the training that cultivate the knowledge of various technologies as they are used in teaching and learning settings, and conversely, knowing how science and mathematics teaching might change as the result of using particular technologies seem to be inevitable.

3.3 TPACK Competencies for Pre-service Science and Mathematics Teachers

At present, researchers (cf. LeBaron, McDonough& Robinson, 2009; Kirschner, Wubbels & Brekelmans, 2008; Mcdougall, 2008) are questioning the efficacy of teacher preparation for successful use of technology in schools and classrooms. LeBaron et al. (2009) believe that the quality of teaching with technology depends in some significance measures on the way teachers were taught to work with technology. There are still some challenges on how teachers are trained to integrate technology with pedagogy and content. Studies by Pope, Hare, & Howard (2002) and Selinger (2001) cited in Angeli (2005) found that preservice teacher education does not adequately prepare future teachers to teach with technology. In most teachers training colleges the concept of TPACK is still new, thus preservice teachers are still learning technology, pedagogy and content as independent subjects; not as integrated knowledge.

11

In this way, teachers have been prepared to teach technology rather than using technology to enhance students' learning (Beyerbach et al., 2001; Jimoyiannis, 2010; Schmidt et al, 2009).

According to Beyerbach et al. (2001) and UNESCO (2008a) teachers should not only be taught how to teach ICT to students but how ICT can help them to teach and enhance students' learning. College instructors are argued to change their views on technology integration, from thinking they would teach about technology, to thinking they would use technology to support preservice teachers learning (Beyerbach et al, 2001; Kirschner et al, 2008; Knezek, Christensen & Fluke, 2003; Mcdougall, 2008; UNESCO, 2008a, 2008b; Webb, 2008). Beyerbach and colleagues further argue for technology integration in teacher education to provide preservice teachers with hands-on experiences, exploring computer technologies and their applications in teaching and learning. In this regard, teacher education is supposed to provide educational courses that model technology integration, field experiences in technology rich classrooms; and a rich, constructivist vision of technology infusion possibilities. Preservice teachers engaging in learning that is rich in hands on activities such as designing of a technology rich lesson and microteaching that involves the use of technology, can develop ability to preservice teachers to demonstrate different technology integration competencies which make up TPACK (Kilic, 2010; Niess et al, 2009; Peker, 2009; UNESCO, 2008a).

UNESCO (2008a) presents competencies in content, technology, pedagogy and profession development required by teachers to develop technological pedagogical content knowledge. Such competencies include: the ability to manage information, structure problem tasks, and integrate open-ended software tools. Also the ability to integrate subject-specific applications with student-centered teaching methods as well as collaborative projects in support of students' deep understanding of key concepts and their application to solve complex, real-world problems (UNESCO, 2008a). Recent calls for educational reform in teacher education stress the need for education restructuring to ensure that preservice teachers not only understand how to use a computer but also how to design high quality technology-enhanced lessons (Niess et al., 2009). According to UNESCO, teachers should be able to use network resources to help students collaborate, access information, and communicate with external experts to analyze and solve their selected problems. More over, teachers are supposed to be able to use ICT to create and monitor individual and group student project plans, as well as collaborate with other teachers and experts in supporting their own professional development. Table 2 presents the training requirements for teachers to develop technological pedagogical content knowledge (UNESCO, 2008a).

Table 2: *Teacher Training Requirement for Developing TPACK Competencies (UNESCO, 2008a)*

Competency area	Training goals	Expected teachers' competencies
Curriculum and assessment	Improve basic literacy skills through technology and adding development of ICT skills into relevant contexts, which will involve time in the curricula of other subjects for the incorporation of a range of relevant ICT resources.	Teachers must have a firm knowledge of the curriculum standards for their subjects, as well as knowledge of standard assessment procedures. In addition, teachers must be able to integrate the use of technology and technology standards for students into the curriculum content.
Pedagogy	Changes in pedagogical practice involve the integration of various technologies, tools, and e-content as part of whole class, group, and individual student activities to support didactic instruction.	Teachers must know where, when (as well as when not), and how to use technology for classroom activities and presentations. Teachers must have the skills to help students create, implement, and monitor project plans and solutions.

ICT	The technologies involved in this approach include the use of computers along with learning software; drill and practice, tutorial, and web content; and the use of networks for management purposes.	Teachers must know basic hardware and software operations, as well as productivity applications software, a web browser, communications software, presentation software, and management applications. Teachers must also be aware of a variety of subject specific tools and applications and able to flexibly use them in teaching.
Teacher professional development	The implications of this approach for teacher training focus on the development of digital literacy and the use of TPACK framework for professional improvement.	Teachers must have the technological skill and knowledge of Web resources necessary to use technology to acquire additional subject matter and pedagogical knowledge in support of teachers' own professional development.

According to UNESCO (2008a), on top of technological, pedagogical and content knowledge there is professional development. Preservice teachers are argued to engage in continuous learning that is geared towards advancing their career development and deepen their understanding about teaching with technology. Teachers' are argued to develop an understanding of how ICT is integrated in teaching to enhance learning rather than how students can learn ICT as a subject (Beyerbach et al, 2001; Jimoyiannis, 2010). The more competent is the teacher, the more he becomes interested, motivated and confident to use technology in teaching (Cox et al, 1999; Kirschners et al, 2008). Research has shown that, teachers uptake of ICT in teaching is highly impaired by the worry of loosing ones self esteem, fear to damage the computer, unfriendly jargon and the likely that the technology may go wrong (Cox et al., 1999; Kirschner et al, 2008; Jimoyiannis, 2010; Webb, 2008; Unwin, 2005). Thus, the question of what and how teachers should learn from the college in order to develop appropriate technology integration competencies should be given the primary focus in studying how technology enhances learning.

3.4 TPACK Training Package for Preservice Teachers

In order to move from teaching technology to using technology to enhance teaching, teachers should be prepared to see technology as part and parcel of their daily classroom activities. The way prospective teachers are set to interact with technology can help to transform their thinking about technology and be able to use it to support students' learning. Beyerbach et al. (2001) and UNESCO (2008b) propose different dosages required by preservice teachers at the college in order to develop the appropriate competencies for integrating technology, pedagogy and content. If these activities are properly adopted in the teachers training colleges, preservice teachers are likely to develop the required technological pedagogical content knowledge and thus be able to apply TPACK in their teaching. Table 3, shows the different training activities for developing preservice teachers competencies in TPACK.

Table 3: *Technological Infusion Activities for Preservice Teachers* (Beyerbach et al., 2001; ISTE, 2008; UNESCO, 2008b)

Competency areas	Training goals	Training activities
Curriculum and Assessment	Teachers should be able to; identify key characteristics of classroom practices and help students to acquire ICT skills within the context of their subjects. They should also be able to use ICT to assess students' acquisition of subject matter and provide feedback on their progress	Select subject-specific software packages and identify specific curriculum standards that are associated with these packages Prepare a lesson plan that includes the use of ICT, such as word processors, web browsers, email, blogs, wikis, and other technologies Incorporate ICT and other software for formative and summative assessment into their lesson plans
Pedagogy	Teacher should be able to: Use didactic teaching and ICT to support students' learning, design appropriate ICT activities to support students' learning. Also use presentation software and digital resources to support instruction.	Use of ICT to support students' learning and demonstrate how technology can supplement didactic classroom teaching. Design lessons that incorporate tutorial and drill and practices, e-resources and e-content and have participants share these plans and receive recommendations from peers.
ICT	Describe the internet and the World Wide Web; elaborate their uses, and how a browser works. Describe the function of tutorial and drill and practice software and how they support students' learning. Use common communication and collaboration technologies, such as text messaging, video conferencing, and web-based collaboration and social environments	Discuss the purpose of internet and WWW and have participants use a browser to access popular websites Demonstrate variety of tutorial and drill and practice packages in the subject domains of the participants and describe how they support students' learning. Discuss the advantages communication and collaboration technologies and have participants use these technologies to communicate and collaborate with others
Teacher Professional Development	Use ICT resources to support their own acquisition of subject matter and pedagogical knowledge	Discuss different ICT resources that participants can use to increase their subject matter and pedagogical knowledge

As presented in Table 3, it is important for technological courses to be linked to methodological courses and field experiences to let the prospective teachers witness firsthand how technology can be effectively integrated in their teaching (Polly, Mims, Shepherd and Inan, 2009). The development of technological, pedagogical and content knowledge, in the process of teachers' preparations as discussed by Beyerbach et al. (2001), Polly et al. (2009) and UNESCO (2008a & b) affirms the use of TPACK as a framework for teachers' preparation. Groth, Spickler, Bergner, Bardzell (2009) call for teachers to engage with content, pedagogy, and technology in tandem to develop knowledge of how technology can help students learn specific science and mathematics concepts. Teachers are argued to develop sufficient knowledge of the curriculum standards for their subjects, standards for assessment procedures and develop sufficient knowledge for integrating the use of technology and technology standards for students in the curriculum (UNESCO, 2008a). According to the skills standards for ICT integration in teaching, set by UNESCO teachers are also expected to develop knowledge on where, when (as well as when not) and how to use technology for classroom activities and presentations.

3.5 Summary and Way Forward

UNESCO (2008b) proposes a number of training activities that can cultivate teachers' knowledge in subject matter, pedagogy and technology. Such activities include; preservice teachers' participation in the preparation of ICT integrated lesson as well as teachers' opportunity to demonstrate the use of technology in a situation similar to real teaching. Jimoyiannis (2010) supports this argument by showing how preservice teachers can develop technology integration competency through an integrated framework which combines TPACK model and authentic learning activities. According to Jimoyiannis (2010), if preservice teachers are willing to learn and develop new skills related to their instruction, it is reasonable to engage them in solving meaningful instruction problems through authentic ICT-based learning activities with a sound pedagogical background.

Studies by Harris & Hofer (2009), Kilic (2010) and Peker (2009) confirm that, when teachers engage in authentic activities such as microteaching and lesson designs, which reflect the real teaching, they get an opportunity to develop skills in drawing learners' attention, asking questions, using and managing time effectively and bringing the lesson to a conclusion. Also by engaging in authentic activities, preservice teachers acquire the skills to choose appropriate technologies to support certain learning activities and overcome difficulties encountered during the teaching process. According to Kilic (2010), teacher candidates can also improve their skills in giving feedback and measurement and evaluation when they engage in a field related activities. This proposes an approach in which preservice teachers design an authentic teaching activity and present to peers in a way similar to real classroom teaching. The challenges that a preservice teacher may get from peers can help him to reflect the similar challenges he may experience in a real teaching (Peker, 2009). According to Peker (2009), preservice teachers should engage in the designing of a technology rich lesson, present to peers (Microteaching), discussion with peers the outcomes of the presentation (critiques), redesign the lesson incorporating the ideas raised by peers during discussion, re-presentation of the lesson to the same group (peer group) for further critiques (evaluation). The process is cyclic as shown in Figure 1.

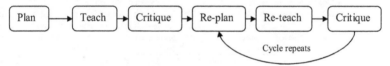

Figure 1: TPACK Training Cycles Adopted at DUCE (adapted from Peker, 2009)

According to Peker (2009) the cycles can be repeated as many times as possible depending on the ability of the preservice teachers to demonstrate the required competencies. A group failing to demonstrate ability in the integration of technology, pedagogy and content, and thus less competent in technological pedagogical content knowledge, may be required to redesign the lesson and present to peers again and again until the three elements of TPACK are well integrated in their teaching. The approach is considered effective in developing teachers' competencies for teaching science and mathematics with technology and thus enhancing performance outcomes in these subjects.

Chapter Four

Research Methodology

This chapter presents the design of the research and the methods used in collecting data. It comprises of six sections (4.1 to 4.6). Section 4.1 presents the research design where as section 4.2 describe the participants' characteristics. The chapter also presents the instruments used for data collection in section 4.3, the interventions carried out during the study in section 4.4 and data collection procedures in section 4.5. The data analysis approach is presented in section 4.6.

4.1 Research Design

This study employed an action based research design. According to Mertler (2006), action research is a research method intended to solve practical problems of an individual or a group or an institution through planned intervention in the day-to-day working practice. This approach was used at DUCE in order to improve preservice teachers' competencies in technology integration in teaching by developing an understanding of technology, pedagogy and content and its integration in teaching to form TPACK (cf. Grundy & Kemmis, 1982). The study employed the pre and post interventions analysis of preservice teachers' competency of integrating technology, pedagogy and content. Adopting the approach used by Howden (1998) and Lundeberg, Bergland, Klyczek & Hoffman (2003), prior to intervention, preservice teachers participated in a survey and microteaching which were aimed at identifying their competency in technology integration in teaching. This was followed by a TPACK training and discussion with peers, which enabled them to identify weaknesses in their technological integration in teaching. Based on the technological weaknesses identified during the discussion, preservice teachers developed alternative approaches to enhance the integration of technology, pedagogy and content in teaching. The new approaches guided them in the re-design of the lesson which was later on presented to colleagues for the second time. At the end of intervention, preservice teachers participated in another survey and reflection on the intervention activities carried out during the study. It was expected that by the end of the intervention both instructors and preservice teachers at DUCE would adopt a new teaching and learning approach that incorporate TPACK as a basic framework for lessons that integrate technology.

4.2 Participants

Four instructors from the department of curriculum and teaching and 29 pre-service science and mathematics teachers participated in the intervention. College instructors were involved in the study in order to provide an overview of the preservice teachers' preparation processes. Their information was useful in substantiating the data collected from questionnaire and observation checklist. Instructors also provided the basis for the advice of necessary measures to be taken to overcome the existing incompetency of preservice teachers' in TPACK. However, the large part of the study involved students in the Bachelor of Education in Science {B.Ed (science)}, who discussed the technology integration weaknesses and explored the best way they can integrate technology in their teaching. Participants were taken as "a case" for the study because by the time the study was conducted, they were in their last month of their bachelors' program. Thus, were expected to demonstrate an exemplary competence level that all preservice teachers do acquire at DUCE. Also B.Ed (science) program includes students who specialized in mathematics, chemistry, physics and biology, which were the focus subjects in this study (i.e. science and mathematics). Table 4 presents the demographic characteristic of the participants in this study.

Table 4: *Demographic Characteristics of Participants*

Participants	Gender		Age	Teaching Experience		Teaching Subject				Computer use		
	M	F		Yes	No	Mat	Ph	Chem	Bi	Always	1/week	Rarely
Students 29	26	3	20-36	21	8	10	10	1	8	10	10	9
Instructors 4	3	1	34-42	4	0	1	1	0	2	4	0	0

4.3 Instruments

Four kinds of data collection instruments were used in the study: a student questionnaire, Researcher log book, an instructor interview and an observation checklist.

4.3.1 Student Questionnaire

Questionnaires had items related to all three research questions covered in this study. The same questionnaire was used for pre and post-intervention assessment of preservice teachers' competency in technology and its integration with pedagogy and content. The change in technological pedagogical content knowledge was measured from the difference between pre-intervention and post intervention survey results. In addition, there was a reflection questionnaire; it comprised of both closed and open ended questions related to second and third research questions. All questionnaires were adopted from Schmidt et al. (2009) and the Organization for Economic Co-operation and Development (OECD) (2009). Questions from Schmidt et al (i.e. TPACK survey questions) had the reliability value between 0.75 and 0.92 Cronbach's alpha, and were used to measure the knowledge on TPACK. OECD questionnaire had no specified reliability value, but were relevant in the investigation of technological competencies and pedagogical use of ICT (**see Appendix A, for the complete questionnaire**).

4.3.2 Instructors' Interview

Interview questions were prepared to gather information on how college instructors integrate ICT in their classroom and the extent to which their ICT integration can be adopted by preservice teachers. Through interview it was also possible to gather information about the instructors' technological pedagogical content knowledge and whether their knowledge was a replica to preservice teachers. In addition, interviews were important in establishing the relationship between what preservice teachers learn from their instructors and what they can be able to demonstrate in teaching. Understanding of this concept was important in establishing the reason for inadequate or adequate use of ICT in teaching among preservice teachers. All interview questions were semi structured with open ended questions, modified from UNESCO (2008a) and Schmidt et al (2009) (see **Appendix B for the complete interview questions**).

4.3.3 Observation checklist

Data were also collected by using an observation checklist based on the technological standards of ISTE (2008), Schmidt et al (2009) and UNESCO (2008a). However, not all items from ISTE, Schmidt et al and UNESCO were used as they are. There are some items which were dropped and some were modified to fit the context of DUCE and objectives of this study. The observation checklist was used to investigate the way preservice teachers were working with ICT during microteaching, lesson design, and during the presentation of the lesson with TPACK framework. The observation checklist used during the pre-intervention to assess the level of technology integration competencies among preservice teachers, was also used in the post-intervention to asses the change in technology integration competencies (see **Appendix C for the complete observation checklist**).

4.3.4 Researcher's Log Book

The researchers' log book was used to maintain a record of activities and events occurring during the intervention process, which could not be recorded by using observation checklist. Thus, researcher's log book was used during peer appraisal, TPACK training and lesson design. Data collected through this method were important in describing the interventions processes.

Table 5: *Summary of Data Collection Instrument for Each Research Theme*

Research Theme	Data Collection Instruments			
	Student questionnaire	Researcher Log book	Teacher interview	Observation checklist
ICT competencies	√	√		√
Practices to enhance TPACK	√	√	√	√
Developed competencies in TPACK	√		√	√

4.4 Intervention

Five intervention activities were planned for the project. Microteaching was one of the interventions designed for preservice teachers. Preservice teachers, in a group of seven prepared a short lesson and presented to peers. Training on TPACK was another component of the intervention, followed by peer appraisal. After the peer appraisal preservice teachers engaged in the process of designing a lesson that incorporates ideas discussed during the peer appraisal. The designed lesson was finally presented and discussed with peers. At the end of the project, preservice teachers had an opportunity to reflect on the intervention activities carried out during the TPACK project.

4.4.1 Microteaching

In a group of seven, preservice teachers designed and presented a technology integrated lesson to their colleagues (microteaching). The microteaching was conducted in computer lab, to allow preservice teachers who prepared a computer based instruction to have access to computers. Data were collected by using an observation checklist which was rated by peer students and the researcher. During observation, attention was paid on how preservice teachers were using technology to facilitate learning. Each presentation was video taped to ease the reflection during the peer discussion which followed after microteaching. The discussion was aimed to assess the preservice teachers' knowledge of integrating technology, pedagogy and content to form TPACK. At this moment the discussion was not successful because most of the preservice teachers had no idea about TPACK. Thus, training was conducted to introduce the concept of TPACK.

4.4.2 Training about TPACK

During the training, different kinds of ICTs that can support learning were discussed; example iPod, Camera, Wikipedia, Online games, Blogs, Television, Computer, MP3, e-portfolios, discussion forums, Course Management Systems and mobile phones. Using the concepts of Koehler & Mishra (2009), preservice teachers and the researcher discussed the concept of TPACK with attention to; the representation of concepts using pedagogical techniques that use technologies in constructive ways to teach content. The training also paid attention on the knowledge of what makes concepts difficult or easy to learn and how technology can help readdress some of the problems that students face. Preservice teachers also learned the importance of understanding the context; example, understanding the students' prior knowledge on how technology can be used to build on existing knowledge to develop new knowledge. During the training, data were collected by using a researcher's log book, in which a researcher was recording all new ideas raising up during the training; example challenges that can be encountered when integrating technology, pedagogy and content. Through out the training, the researcher was using log book to record the learning difficulties that preservice teachers were experiencing, preservice teachers' opinions and attitude about the use of TPACK and possible opportunities and limitations in the use of TPACK for their learning.

4.4.3 Peers' Appraisal

At the end of the training preservice teachers engaged in a discussion to reflect on the microteaching in relation to TPACK training. In the discussion preservice teachers analyzed the video recorded during microteaching to identify weaknesses and strengths of their teaching with technology, in relation to what they learned about TPACK. From the video, preservice teachers could easily identify some weakness in their integration of technology pedagogy and content. The following are examples of the weaknesses identified from the first microteaching by preservice teachers:

1. All presentation used only Power Point, which was said to be not enough in enhancing learning (no difference between power point and lecture). The use of PowerPoint to present text information was reported to have no impact to the students' learning, unless it comprised some illustrative pictures. Thus, it was proposed that, technology use should allow students participation in the learning with technology and not only a teacher using technology to present the concept.
2. The pedagogy was not clear during the presentation. Almost all groups used discussion method which was challenged for being difficult to integrate with technology. The choice of a pedagogical approach that is appropriate for a given technology was also found to be difficult to them. And thus proposed the adoption of constructivist learning approaches.
3. Although preservice teachers had basic knowledge of technology, pedagogy and content, during the presentation, there interplay between technology pedagogy and content was a missing. Preservice teachers argued that from all presentation it was hard to identify the point of integration between technology, pedagogy and content to form TPACK. Instead there was TK, PK, CK, TCK and PCK in all presentation it was impossible to see the combination of TPK and TPACK. During the presentation, preservice teachers used technology and pedagogy separately to present the content (see Figure 2).

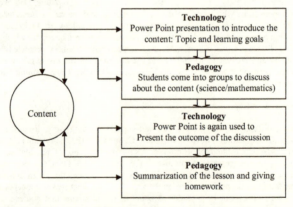

Figure 2: The missing interplay between technology, pedagogy and content

19

As an outcome of the discussion, preservice teachers developed some questions which were considered as guidelines to the design of the lesson that integrate technology pedagogy and content. Such questions include:

1. What to take into account when preparing a technology supported instruction?
   Suggested answers
   a. Teacher and student prior knowledge (context)
   b. Social construct (context)
   c. Learning approaches; Problem based, Inquiry learning, Task based, Collaborative learning (use of constructivist learning approach)
   d. Choice of technology in relation to pedagogy and content

2. How to use technology in the process of teaching and learning?
   Possible solutions
   a. Teachers use technology to deliver a lesson to student?
   b. Teachers guide students to work with technology?
   c. Both teacher and students work collaboratively using technology?
   d. Use social learning communities such as moodle, teletop, Elgg and blogs?

3. In integrating technology, pedagogy and content; what should start first?
   Possible solutions
   a. Start with content (choose the topic then think of pedagogy and technology)
   b. Its better to think for the kind of technology you have before you decide on what to teach
   c. Because what you are supposed to teach is fixed, its important to think how you can support what is already in the syllabus, so better choose the content and think of what technology to support the content.

These questions acted as important guideline in the re-designing of the lesson.

4.4.4 Design of the Lesson

Four groups of 7 preservice teachers were made; each had the freedom to choose any science or mathematics topic of interest. There was one group in each subject except for the chemistry subject which had only one preservice teacher specializing in chemistry. Thus the preservice teacher from chemistry subject was to work with the Physics group. Also about half of the participants in the study were mathematics preservice teachers. Due to their number, they were allowed to make two groups. Therefore, there was one group for physics, one group for biology and two groups for Mathematics (see Table 6).

Table 6: *Groups Participated in the Design of the Lesson*

Group	Subject	Learning activity
Group No. 1	Physics	Simulations of simple pendulum. Determining the relationship between angle of release, length, time and number of oscillations
Group No. 2	Mathematics	Calculation of radius and diameter: Using different mathematics symbols available in the computer to draw and calculate radius and diameter given that π is constant.
Group No. 3	Mathematics	Using charts to presents statistical data: using tabular data to create a chart or graph by using excel.
Group No. 4	Biology	Simulations DNA coding: observing the interaction between ribosome RNA, transfer RNA and messenger RNA.

In groups, preservice teachers designed a lesson that incorporates TPACK. Their design was guided by the questions developed during the discussion (after microteaching). Throughout the lesson design process, the researcher was playing a role of an observer, facilitator, guide and a teacher. In some instances the researcher played a role of a consultant. During the lesson design, data were collected through the researcher's log book, where records of the design process were put on the log book.

4.4.5 Presentation of the Lesson

After the lesson design, the researcher, preservice teachers and four instructors joined in the presentation of the designed lesson. During presentation; the researcher and preservice teachers engaged in the process of evaluating the presentation by using observation checklists. The same observation checklist used in the first microteaching was also used in the presentation of the designed lesson. Different from the first presentation (microteaching) in which preservice teachers used mainly PowerPoint for presentations of the lesson; in the second presentation about four programs were used: simulation, Microsoft Word, Excel and PowerPoint. Example, the physics group simulated the simple pendulum, assessing the change in number of oscillations in relation to the change of time. The biology group simulated the DNA coding, describing the working of tRNA, mRNA and rRNA. One of the mathematics groups used Excel to demonstrate the drawing of mathematical graphs, and the other mathematics group used Microsoft Word program to draw circles in Mathematics. As it was for microteaching, this presentation was followed by a discussion with peers. A researcher, invited college instructors and preservice teachers, participated in this discussion which granted an opportunity for preservice teachers to share what they observed from the presentation.

4.4.6 Reflection

At the end of the intervention, two kinds of questionnaire were administered to preservice teachers; the TPACK survey questionnaire and the reflection questionnaire. These questionnaires were administered to inquire the preservice teachers' experience in working with TPACK. In this survey preservice teachers had the opportunity to express what they learned and possibilities and limitations they can experience in using TPACK framework to enhance their teaching. The reflection questions also considered the preservice teachers' attitude towards ICT integration in science and mathematics teaching. All the activities carried out during the study are summarized in Table 7.

Table 7: *Interventions Activities and Data collection Instrument during TPACK Project*

Interventions	Activity	Objective	Instrument
Before intervention	Survey	To asses technology integration competencies: Knowledge, Skills and Attitudes towards ICT and its integration with pedagogy and content	Student's Questionnaire Instructors' interview
Intervention	Microteaching	To assess ICT integration competencies and technological pedagogical content knowledge.	Observation checklist, video recording
	Peers' appraisal	Peers assessment and critiques on the strength and weaknesses of presentation (microteaching)	Researcher's log book
	Training on TPACK	Introducing the concept of TPACK to pre-service science and mathematics teachers	Researcher's log book
	Design of a lesson	To develop preservice teachers' ability to use ICT in teaching and TPACK competencies. In group of 7, redesigned a lesson presented during microteaching.	Researcher's log book

	Presentation of the lesson in the class	Assess if there was any change in technology integration and TPACK competency. Discuss and choose the exemplary design to be used in schools	Observation checklist Video recording of presentations
	Peer appraisal	Sharing the improvements from the previous presentation, challenges and failures	Researcher's log book
Post intervention	1. Reflection 2. Survey	Assess change in knowledge about TPACK and readiness to integrate technology in teaching.	Questionnaire: closed and open ended questions

4.5 Data Collection Procedures

There were three data collection procedures employed during the study as adopted from Best & Khan (2006). Best & Khan, describe data collection methods as different methods and procedures developed to aid in the acquisition of data. Thus, in this study different methods were employed for data collections, including questionnaire method (personally administered questionnaires), interview method (semi structured interview) and observation method (overt observation approach). The different research methods were used in different stages of the study; starting with the pre-intervention (Questionnaire, interview and observation), during intervention (observation) and post intervention process (questionnaire and observation). Use of more than one instrument to collect data that can answer the same question was considered important for the triangulation of data. For example, findings from college instructors' interview were used for cross examining the results of the findings from student questionnaire and observation checklist.

4.6 Data Analysis

Quantitative data from questionnaires and observation checklist were analyzed by computing means and standard deviations. Also two paired sample t-test was used to find out if there was statistically significant difference between the preservice teachers' knowledge on TPACK before intervention and after intervention. Pearson correlation coefficient was also used to find out if there was statistically significant relationship between technological knowledge and use of technology in learning and accessibility to technology. On the other hand, qualitative data were analyzed by using interaction matrix and contact summary sheet. The interaction matrix is used to establish the combination, interaction or influence of one parameter on another parameter within the system (Mavroulidou, Hughes & Hellawell, 2004). The size of the matrix, therefore, is determined by the number of parameters selected by respondents (see Table 26, p. 38). Summary sheet refers to a single sheet, with some focusing or summarizing questions about a particular field contact (Miles & Huberman, 1994). The summary sheet had the questions and summary of response of each interviewee (see Table 8).

Table 8: *Contact Summary Sheet for Analysis of Qualitative Data*

Interview questions	Summary of responses			
	Interviewee 1	Interviewee 2	Interviewee 3	Interviewee 4
Question 1				
Question 2				
Question 3				
Question 4				

Recorded audio information were transcribed and sorted according to their relevance to the research questions presented in the summary sheet.

4.6.1 Instruments' Validity

All instruments were evaluated by three experts: one from the University of Twente, doing research on TPACK and teaching courses related to education technology and two from the University of Dar es salaam who are also doing research in educational technology and teaching ICT Courses. The evaluation of the instrument by experts led to the change of the observation checklist scales; from continuous scales (0 to 10) to categorical scales (Yes or No). Questions about technological tools used in the preservice teachers learning at the college were modified to exclude all tools that were not available at the college such as interactive whiteboard. Questions adopted from Schmidt et al (2009) were not changed.

4.6.2 Reliability Analysis

All data collected through questionnaires and observation checklists were subjected to reliability analysis to test their consistency. The cronbach's alpha value for the reliability of data collected through student questionnaire (before intervention) with a scale of five points, with 1= *strongly disagree* and 5 = *strongly agree,* was 0.84. The reliability for data collected through questionnaire after intervention was 0.81 cronbach's alpha. Questions from observation checklist before intervention had a cronbach's alpha value of 0.68 and after intervention was 0.71, and was having a scale of 2 points with 1 = *Yes* and 2 = *No*. The reliability for data collected on the students' reflection about the project was 0.86 cronbach's alpha and had a scale of 5 points similar to those in the questionnaires. A sample reliability values for each TPACK variables from the pre-intervention questionnaire are summarized in Table 9.

Table 9: *Reliability Values for each TPACK Variable in TPACK Survey*

Variable	Schmidt's Cronbach's Alpha	Observed Cronbach's Alpha
Technological knowledge	0.82	0.77
Pedagogical Knowledge	0.84	0.84
Content Knowledge (Mathematics)	0.85	0.81
Content Knowledge (Physics)	0.82	0.82
Content Knowledge (Chemistry)	0.82	Not computed
Content knowledge (Biology)	0.82	0.92
Pedagogical Content Knowledge	0.85	0.71
Technological Content Knowledge	0.80	0.85
Technological Pedagogical Knowledge	0.86	0.84
Technological Pedagogical and content Knowledge	0.92	0.75

The reliability values presented in Table 9 were found to be sufficient in deriving an inference of this study. Data collected in this study were considered reliable because their reliability values were close to those of Schmidt et al (2009), where the questionnaire was adopted.

Chapter Five

Findings

This chapter presents the findings from the study as were obtained from preservice teachers at DUCE. The findings are presented on the basis of the research questions answered in this study; the first question was related to competencies that pre-service science and mathematics teachers at DUCE have in relation to the use of ICT in teaching and is presented in section 5.1. The second question was about practices which are effective in improving preservice teachers' ability to integrate technology with content and pedagogy at DUCE and is presented in section 5.2. The last question was about the impacts of TPACK interventions on improving the pre-service science and mathematics teachers' ability to use TPACK framework which is presented in section 5.3.

5.1 Preservice teachers Competency in the Use of ICT in Teaching

Preservice teachers' competency in ICT use was investigated through the assessment of ICT use in the courses they attended at the college, accessibility to various ICT tools at the college, and their ability to use Web 2.0 tools in their learning. In assessing this competency, mainly three methods were used: the survey method (using the student questionnaire), microteaching (using an observation checklist) and an interview with college instructors, which was carried out to assess the extent to which they were using ICT in the training of the preservice teachers at the college and the extent to which their technological integration was replica to preservice teachers' technological integration competencies.

ICT Use at the College

In an analysis of the extent to which different technological tools were used in different courses, it was revealed that the use of audio equipments and the use of digital photo camera were the lowest with values below the mean in a scale of 6 points where 1 = *"Never"*, 2 = *"rarely"*, 3 = *"Less than half a time"* 4 = *"half the time"*, 5 = *"more than half the time"* and 6 = *"Almost always"*. Other technological tools such as computer, learning management system, projection system and mobile phone were having values which were slightly below the mean (see Table 10). The overall use of ICT at the college was low ($M = 2.956$ and $SD = 1.020$), which implies a low level of technology use in different courses offered at the college.

Table 10: *Use of Technological Tools in Courses Undertaken by Preservice Teachers at the College*

Technological Tool	Mean	Std. Deviation
Use of Personal Computers	3.34	1.72
Use of Learning management system	3.17	1.79
Use of Audio equipment	2.66	1.74
Use of Digital photo camera	1.59	1.38
Use of Mobile Phones	3.45	2.18
Projection systems	3.48	1.72
Television	3.00	2.20

$N = 29$

As it is presented in Table 10, there was a high standard deviation for the use of all technological tools, with television and mobile phones having the highest standard deviations. This implies that, preservice teachers had different opinions on the usability of these tools; whereby some of them reports to be using while others report to have not used. The disparity in the use of ICT tools in the learning process was thought to be caused by the differences in accessibility to those learning tools.

Accessibility to technological tools

Results showed that, with exception of audio equipments (mp3, mp4 and iPod), digital camera and television, the rest of technological tools were either within or above the mean. Computer was found to be more accessible than other technological tools; having the highest mean and the lowest standard deviation in a 3 points scale where 1 = *Not available*, 2 = *restricted access* and 3 = *free access* (Table 11). The overall mean for the accessibility to technological tools lied between unavailability and restricted access (M = 1.877, SD = 0.40), meaning that most of technological tools were either unavailable or had restricted accessibility.

Table 11: *Accessibility to Various Technological Tools at the College*

Technological Tool	Mean	Std. Deviation
Access to PC (computer lab)	2.34	0.55
Access to learning management systems	2.21	0.86
Access to audio equipments	1.34	0.67
Access to digital photo camera	1.24	0.58
Access to mobile phones	2.03	0.94
Access to projection systems	2.00	0.54
Access to television	1.97	0.82

N = 29

As it is indicated in Table 11, the low access to various technological tools that support learning is considered to have affected the opportunity of the preservice teachers to use technological tools to support their learning. However, the accessibility analysis show that, preservice teachers had more access to computer and learning management system than other ICT tools such as audio equipments, television, projection systems and camera.

Use of Web 2.0

An analysis of the use of Web 2.0 facilities to support learning revealed that, only the use of Google search engine and email were above the mean in a 5 points scale, where 1 = *never*, 2 = *occasionally*, 3 = *sometimes*, 4 = *oftenly* and 5 = *always*. Google search engine was having the highest mean and lowest standard deviation. Other web 2.0 facilities, including social learning communities (facebook, blogs and wikis) were below the mean and having high standard deviations. The overall mean and standard deviation values for the use of various Web 2.0 facilities was M = 2.43, SD = 0.63, which imply that preservice teachers' use of Web 2.0 facilities was lying between occasionally and sometimes, which is not sufficient enough to enhance preservice teachers' development of technology integration competencies.

Table 12: *Use of Web 2.0 to Support Learning*

Web 2.0	Mean	Std. Deviation
Use of Google as search engine	4.17	0.76
Use of wikis	1.76	1.15
Use of weblogs	2.07	1.03
Use of social learning communities e.g. facebook	1.69	1.20
Use of email	3.03	1.38
Chat	1.83	1.04

N = 29

A correlation analysis between the use of technology, accessibility to technology and the use of Web 2.0 tools was carried out to assess the impact each component was having to the other. Findings from the Pearson's correlation, revealed a significant positive correlation $(r\ (29) = 0.61,\ P = 0.00)$ between accessibility and use of technological tools. This implies that, the more preservice teachers could access technological tools, the more likely they could use those tools in learning. Also there was a significant relationship between use of technological tools and the use of web 2.0 facilities $(r\ (29) = 0.40,\ P = 0.02)$. This also means that those who were able to use technological tools are the one who could also use Web 2.0 tools for their learning. But there was no relationship between accessibility to technological tools and use of web 2.0 facilities, which implies that, the accessibility to technological tools, did not guarantee use of web 2.0 facilities. Preservice teachers' use of Web 2.0 facilities was highly determined by the technological use rather than accessibility to technological tools.

Technological knowledge

During the TPACK survey, it was found that technological knowledge of the preservice teachers was average, having values slightly above the mean, in a 5 points scale, where 1 = *Strongly Disagree* and 5 = *Strongly Agree*. Preservice teachers reported to have limited opportunity to work with technology at the college. In addition, mean values indicated that preservice teachers were not sure if they can use technology without problem, learn technology easily and if they had technological skills to be able to use technology (Table 13).

Table 13: *Preservice teachers' Technological Knowledge*

Technological Knowledge	Mean	Std. Deviation
I can use technology without problems	3.34	0.86
I can learn technology easily	3.55	0.91
I have the technical skills, I need to use technology	3.59	1.02
I have sufficient opportunity to work with technology	2.66	0.86

$N = 29$

As reported in Table 13, there was high standard deviation in each technological competency item. The high standard deviation entails that, technological knowledge differed greatly among preservice teachers at the colleges.

The extent to which technological tools were used in the course that preservice teachers attended and the extent to which preservice teachers had an access to those tools and the level of use of Web 2.0 tools were thought to have an impact in the development of preservice teachers' technological knowledge. Thus, further analysis was carried out to find out if there was any correlation between the development of technological knowledge and the use of technological tools, access to technological tools as well as the use of web 2.0 facilities.

Results showed a significant positive correlation $(r\ (28) = 0.40,\ P = 0.03)$ between the use of various technological tools and development of technological knowledge. There was also a significant relationship $(r\ (28) = 0.52,\ P = 0.00)$ between the use of web 2.0 tools (wikis, blogs, Facebook, email) and the development of technological knowledge. However, there was insignificant correlation $(r\ (28) = 0.15,\ P = 0.44)$ between accessibility to technological tools and development of technological knowledge. Results imply that, the more preservice teachers had an opportunity to use technological tools in their learning, the more they became competent in technological knowledge. For example, preservice teachers who had an opportunity to use web 2.0 tools for learning and communication had more likelihood of developing technological knowledge than those who were not. This may mean that, access to technology doesn't necessarily enhance technological knowledge rather the extent to which preservice teachers use technology in learning is what matters.

Further more, researches have reported that, the preservice teachers' ability to integrate technology in teaching depends on how they learned to use technology. Thus, an investigation of what preservice teachers can do with technology needs an understanding of how preservice teachers learned to use technology. In this regard, an analysis of how college instructors' use technology in teaching was considered important in deriving an inference on whether the preservice teachers' incompetency in using technology resulted from the way they learned from their instructors or there were other factors. Thus, an interview with instructors was conducted. During interview, college instructors acknowledged the fact that they were not replica to their students (preservice teachers), and were aware that their students were not good enough in using ICT in teaching. All four instructors interviewed, were competent in PCK and had limited knowledge on the integration of TK into PCK. Their responses are summarized Table 14.

Table 14: *Summary of Interview with College Instructors*

Interview question	Summary of responses			
	Interviewee 1	Interviewee 2	Interviewee 3	Interviewee 4
How can you rate your own technological competency?	I have a moderate technological competency. …this is caused by the limited supply of ICT facilities at the college… the college lacks ICT tools such as interactive white board, learning environment etc	…my technological competency is very low. …I don't have knowledge about ICT tools that can facilitate learning. I also don't know the software and some computer programs that I can support learning.	Majority of teachers at this college are missing the skills of using ICT tools. …but I can't say I am excellent, I think I am average	I have moderate competency. …we don't have most of the technological tools here… it becomes very difficult to work with technology.
What do you think about your students' competency on TPACK?	I don't think if they are competent that much. Because the pedagogical part is difficult to measure, where as the other components are featured. For example they can use computer to solve out a content problem. So the two can be easily measured but the pedagogy is a bit complex.	…they learn about ICT. Since they are taught to use ICT in their learning they might be aware of it. But would have learned more if there were sufficient ICT tools. I am worried that the knowledge they get may be difficult to implement in their work, because in their competency is questionable.	…they are weak in technology, so I don't think if it is possible for them to integrate technology pedagogy and content. Because even the computer lab we have is not sufficient to develop technological competency of students.	I don't think if they have such a competency: … the problem is that, students were supposed to learn these things in their methodological courses… but you will find that they are learning only content and pedagogy and not the technology. So its difficult to be competent

College instructors confirmed that the level of technology use at the college is low, leading to low technology integration competencies among preservice teachers. For example, the response by an interviewee number 4 on the second questions shows that there are weaknesses on the courses that preservice teachers attend at the college. Methodological courses which would have integrated the three components of TPACK are focused only on pedagogy and content. As reported by other instructors (interviewee one to three), technological tools and professional development program for instructors are also missing at the college. The limited opportunity for preservice teachers to experience learning with technology, make them unable to develop the technological pedagogical content knowledge. This was proved in an analysis of the preservice teachers' knowledge of technology, pedagogy and content, and the manner they are integrated. In this analysis, reservice teachers agreed to have pedagogy knowledge, content knowledge, pedagogical content knowledge and technological pedagogical knowledge (mean above 4, in a 5 points scale, where 1 = *strongly disagree* and 5 = *strongly agree*) but were undecided on their technological knowledge, technological content knowledge and technological pedagogical content knowledge which had a mean below 4; technological knowledge having the lowest mean value (Table 15).

Table 15: *Competencies in TPACK (Based on TPACK Survey Questionnaire)*

Competency area	Mean	Std. Deviation
Technological Knowledge	3.18	0.65
Pedagogical Knowledge	4.29	0.46
Content knowledge	4.55	0.48
Pedagogical Content Knowledge	4.17	0.57
Technological Content Knowledge	3.54	0.53
Technological Pedagogical Knowledge	4.03	0.67
Technological Pedagogical Content Knowledge	3.46	0.58

N = 29

As reported in Table 15; technological knowledge, technological content knowledge and technological pedagogical content knowledge had the lowest mean, compared to other components. The same was observed during microteaching where only three items (content knowledge, technological pedagogical knowledge and technological content knowledge) were above the mean in a 2 points scales where 1 = *No* and 2 = *Yes* (Table 16).

Table 16: *TPACK Competency as Observed during Microteaching*

	Mean	Std. Deviation
Technological Knowledge	1.50	0.28
Content Knowledge	1.68	0.20
Pedagogical knowledge	1.38	0.27
Technological Pedagogical knowledge	1.54	0.41
Technological Content Knowledge	1.41	0.33
Pedagogical Content Knowledge	1.74	0.32
Technological Pedagogical and Content Knowledge	1.41	0.22

N = 29

These findings suggest that preservice teachers were missing the knowledge of bringing the three components of TPACK together in an integrated manner. This made them incapable to integrate technology pedagogy and content and thus incompetency in TPACK.

5.2 Practices that are Effective in Enhancing Technology Integration Competencies

The second question that this study intended to answer was "what practices are effective in enhancing pre-service science and mathematics teachers' ability to integrate technology, pedagogy and content?" This question was answered by designing a number of hands-on activities (interventions) which were carried out by preservice teachers during the study. The first activity involved the preparation of a microteaching session. This was followed by training on TPACK and peer appraisal on the presentation made during microteaching. The discussion led to the development of guidelines for the redesign of the lesson. Preservice teachers designed a lesson by using TPA CK framework guided by the questions developed during peer appraisal session. They finally presented the designed lesson to peers. The cycle was completed by another peer appraisal, similar to the first microteaching session.

5.2.1 Microteaching (one)

This was done soon after the TPACK survey, and was intended to assess the competency level of preservice teachers in designing and presenting a lesson by using technology. In this practice, preservice teachers in a group of seven, designed a technology supported lesson of their own choice and presented to peers. One of the conditions in the presentation was to ensure that technology, pedagogy and content are properly integrated. Outcome from microteaching revealed that, when preservice teachers were teaching with technology, they paid more attention on technology and content and forgot the pedagogy. This made the pedagogical knowledge to have the lowest mean (refer Table 16). However, the technological knowledge competency was within a mean where as TPACK and TPK were below the mean. It was observed from microteaching that preservice teachers had a limited knowledge of TPACK. Many of them had not even heard the word TPACK. Thus a training to introduce the concept of TPACK was organized.

5.2.2 Training (Introducing the Concept of TPACK)

The training was intended to introduce the concept of TPACK and the meaning of it in teacher education as well as providing tips for the discussion about the microteaching. During the training, varieties of technological and web 2.0 tools that can support learning were discussed, for example; iPod, wikis, online games, blogs, television, computer, mp3, e-portfolio, course management systems, simulations and mobile phones. Procedures for choosing the technological tool in relation to content and pedagogy and its integration in the teaching process, was also discussed. An "aha" effect was observed from preservice teachers when they became aware of the concept of TPACK and the relationship existing between technology pedagogy and content.

5.2.3 Peer appraisal

After the training, preservice teachers engaged in the reflections on the microteaching session. They watched a video of the presentation of each group and had a discussion on the strength and weaknesses of each presentation and ways to improve the technology integration with pedagogy and content. Peers were asking questions and sharing opinions of what and how to improve in the lesson design and presentation.

5.2.4 Design of the Lesson

There were four groups each with seven students, created out of 29 students who participated in the study. These groups were mostly the same as those which participated in the microteaching and thus were required to redesign the lesson they already presented in microteaching. The subject, topic/learning objectives and technology and pedagogy to use were decided by the preservice teachers themselves in their groups. Using a researcher's log book, the researcher was writing down some notice concerning the design process adopted by each group as summarized in Table 17.

Table 17: *Processes taken by each group in the process of designing a lesson*

Group	Design process
Group 1	- They first decided about the technology (Simulation), followed by content (simple pendulum in physics) and finally the pedagogy (task based learning). - It was learned from their design process that, many of the preservice teachers were more worried about technology. Thus, when they meet to discuss what to design they first started thinking about the technology. When they agreed about technology is when they could continue with other components such as technological content, technological pedagogical and pedagogical content knowledge to make technological pedagogical content knowledge. - They had a work sheet (Appendix D), in which the assumed learners were supposed to fill in the change in time, in relation to the change of length of the thread, angle and mass. - In each work sheet there was a task of rating the period against mass, period against angle of release, period against length, and period against acceleration due to gravity - The group was ranked first by peers for its best integration of technology pedagogy and content
Group 2	- Started by identifying the weaknesses in their first presentation (microteaching), followed by discussion on how to correct those weaknesses before they continued to with the design of the lesson. However, this made them to be more focused on the correction of the weaknesses identified from the discussion than new innovations in their lesson - The group considered content as a core of teaching, thus they first thought of the content before all other component of TPACK. Thus they chose "circles topic" in mathematics. - They then thought of the pedagogy (inquiry based learning). The assumed learners were required to draw circles by using a Microsoft Word program and calculate area or circumference for a given a dimensions or radius. Although during the lesson design they proposed the use of tutorial, in the presentation they didn't use the program, instead they used Microsoft Word to draw circles and Microsoft Excels to calculate area, radius etc. - The group was ranked poorest (last) by peers for having unclear integration of technology with content and pedagogy.
Group 3	- Started by identifying challenges that students may encounter in learning with technology - They then chose the technology which is known to many of the students (Excel program). They then thought of the content (statistics; presentation of data by using graphs and charts) which was thought to be relevant to the technology chose. - Finally they discussed the pedagogical approach where they prepared a worksheet, which had all information on what to do, and the procedures to create a graph in excel. The work sheet had several tables with different data and students were asked to present in graphs. - This group was ranked third by the peers; although it presented well but the integration of the three components especially students tasks were not clear.
Group 4	- They first discussed about the technological knowledge of the teachers and students. - Planned a short orientation for students on the use of technology they planed for a lesson. - They then discussed the pedagogical approach before they thought of other components of TPACK. They did this because they were so worried about the constructivist approaches thus they wanted to first be acquainted with it before they continue to other TPACK components (content and technology) which they believed to be aware of. - They then discussed about the technology and agreed to use simulation to teach Genetics (interaction between mRNA, rRNA and tRNA in the DNA coding. - After watching the simulation, students were required to describe the process each RNA component takes before it codes with the other component. - The group was ranked second by the peers; it was agreed that the group made a nice presentation but the component of students watching the presentation of simulation and later on reacting on it was not effective for students' learning.

5.2.5 Lesson Presentation (Microteaching two)

Every group had to present to colleagues what it designed. In the presentation of the lesson, each group had its own route towards an integrated TPACK model. Some started with technology, some with pedagogy and some with content as summarized in Table 17. As it was in the first microteaching, observation checklists were used to indicate the presence or absence of a certain technology integration competency among preservice teachers. Results showed an improved integration of technology, pedagogy and content in the process of teaching. Values for TK, PK, CK, TPK, TCK, PCK and TPACK were all above the mean in a 2 scale points where $1 = No$ and $2 = Yes$. Also all standard deviations were low. See Table 18 for mean values and standard deviations observed during the presentation of the lesson.

Table 18: *Preservice teachers Competency in TPACK as Observed during Presentation*

	Mean	Std. Deviation
Technological Knowledge	1.68	0.26
Content Knowledge	1.62	0.39
Pedagogical knowledge	1.83	0.19
Technological Pedagogical knowledge	1.60	0.38
Technological Content Knowledge	1.60	0.35
Pedagogical Content Knowledge	1.59	0.35
Technological Pedagogical and Content Knowledge	1.60	0.28

N = 39

As presented in Table 18, in the lesson presentation, there was a positive change on the mean values of all components of TPACK, and the standard deviations for all values were lower than the mean, which implies that there was less variability in technology integration competencies among pre-service science and mathematics teachers during the lesson presentation.

In order to identify the kind of activity that was effective in enhancing preservice teachers' technological integration competencies, a reflection questionnaire was administered to preservice teachers who participated in the study. This was intended to inquire the preservice teachers' experience on the intervention activity that had greater impact on their knowledge, skill and insight in working with technology and in developing TPACK competencies.

5.2.6 Reflection on the Project (post intervention)

At the end of the presentation, preservice teachers were given an opportunity to express their experience in working with TPACK by filling in a reflection questionnaire which comprised of both open ended and close ended questions. Preservice teachers had an opportunity to rank their level of achievement in the process of working with TPACK and their view over the whole project. All responses were above the mean (in a 5 point scale, where $1 = strongly\ disagree$ and $5 = strongly\ agree$) (Table 19).

Table 19: *Preservice teachers' Reflection on the Practices that Enhanced on TPACK*

	Mean	Std. Deviation
Microteaching was relevant to my study programme	4.50	0.51
Training session was relevant to my study programme	4.46	0.51
Design of the lesson with TPACK was relevant to my study programme	4.38	0.57
Presentation and peers' appraisal was relevant to my study programme	4.42	0.58
The intervention activities enhanced my technology competency	4.04	0.71
The intervention activities enhanced my pedagogical competency	4.46	0.51
The intervention activities enhanced my competency in content	4.35	0.89
The Microteaching helped me to attain sufficient knowledge about TPACK	4.42	0.50
The training helped me to attain sufficient knowledge about TPACK	4.46	0.71
Peers' appraisal helped me to attain sufficient knowledge about TPACK	4.38	0.64
The lesson design helped me to attain sufficient knowledge about TPACK	4.27	0.60
I attained sufficient insights during microteaching	4.31	0.74
I attained sufficient insight during training session	4.35	0.56
I attained sufficient insight during Lesson Design	4.27	0.45
I attained sufficient insight during discussion with Peers	4.46	0.51
I attained sufficient skills during microteaching	4.23	0.59
I attained sufficient skills during training session	4.42	0.58
I attained sufficient skills during Lesson Design	4.27	0.60
I attained sufficient skills during discussion with Peers	4.50	0.51

N = 26

As presented in Table 19, preservice teachers agreed that all intervention activities were relevant to their study program. They also agreed that the intervention activities enhanced their competency in different TPACK aspects and helped them to attain sufficient knowledge, insights and skills on TPACK. All intervention activities had mean values between 4.0 and 4.5 which imply that majority of preservice teachers "strongly agreed or agreed" on the impact of each item. Also most of the items had low standard deviations (between 0.45 and 0.60). Only four items had high standard deviations (between 0.7 and 0.9) which imply that some preservice teachers did not experience change in their knowledge based on the intervention activities carried out during the study. The highest standard deviation was on the impact of the intervention activities on the content competencies. This is taken as a challenge to the planned interventions as most of the activities carried out during the study were focused on the integration of technology, pedagogy and content and paid less attention on the development of the knowledge of an individual component of TPACK.

5.3 The Impact of the Intervention on TPACK Competency

In order to assess the knowledge change among pre-service science and mathematics teachers in integrating technology pedagogy and content, the questionnaire used during the pre-intervention stage was re-administered in the post intervention stage. Results showed that all responses were above the mean. However, technological knowledge was still having the lowest mean value in a 5 point scales between 1 = *strongly disagree* and 5 = *strongly agree*. Results from the second questionnaire are presented in Table 20.

Table 20: *TPACK Knowledge of the Preservice teachers after the Intervention*

	Mean	Std. Deviation
Technological Knowledge	3.66	0.50
Content Knowledge	4.65	0.32
Pedagogical knowledge	4.66	0.30
Technological Pedagogical knowledge	4.34	0.45
Technological Content Knowledge	4.27	0.43
Pedagogical Content Knowledge	4.35	0.43
Technological Pedagogical and Content Knowledge	4.17	0.38

$N = 22$

A paired sample t-test was conducted to assess the impact of the intervention activities in the development of preservice teachers' competencies in TPACK, between pre-intervention and post-intervention survey results. Results showed a significant change in technological knowledge (TK) between pre and post intervention survey. There was also significant change in technological content knowledge (TCK), technological pedagogical knowledge (TPK) and TPACK. However, the change was insignificant for pedagogical knowledge; content knowledge and pedagogical content knowledge (see Table 21).

Table 21: *Preservice teachers' Pre and Post-intervention TPACK Knowledge*

		Mean	Std. Deviation	Sig.
Pair 1	TK2	3.66	0.50	0.05
	TK1	3.24	0.67	
Pair 2	PK2	4.35	0.32	0.95
	PK1	4.34	0.43	
Pair 3	CK2	4.89	0.24	0.64
	CK1	4.88	0.14	
Pair 6	PCK2	4.34	0.45	0.38
	PCK1	4.20	0.61	
Pair 7	TCK2	4.27	0.43	0.04
	TCK1	3.98	0.57	
Pair 8	TPK2	4.35	0.43	0.05
	TPK1	4.03	0.76	
Pair 9	TPCK2	4.17	0.38	0.02
	TPACK1	3.85	0.51	

$N_1 = 29$, $N_2 = 22$

Although there was a change in the mean values for all variables, t-test results showed insignificant change in some variables as shown in Table 21. These results entail that, preservice teachers already had sufficient knowledge in the three components (content, pedagogy and pedagogical content knowledge) before the intervention. Findings from the pre-intervention survey showed a high mean values for these variables (see mean different from Table 21). Thus, preservice teachers did not experience a significant change in these components which they were already aware of; instead they experienced change in components which they were previously incompetency. This shows that interventions activities carried out during the study successfully cultivated TPACK competencies in areas where there were some weaknesses.

Another paired sample t-test analysis was carried out to find if there was any significant difference between the first microteaching and the second microteaching. Results showed that all components of TPACK except content knowledge were significant at $P < 0.01$ (Table 22). As is the case for the results in Table 21, preservice teachers were already competent in content knowledge, and thus did not significantly change their knowledge in the content areas. However, as reported in Table 19, the project focused less on the development of content knowledge rather the integration of the three is what was given attention during the study.

Table 22: *Paired sample t-test for pre and post-intervention presentation of the lesson*

		Mean	Std. Deviation	Sig
Pair 1	TK1	1.50	0.28	0.00
	TK2	1.68	0.26	
Pair 2	PK1	1.68	0.20	0.00
	PK2	1.82	0.19	
Pair 3	CK1	1.54	0.41	0.10
	CK2	1.61	0.39	
Pair 4	PCK1	1.38	0.27	0.00
	PCK2	1.59	0.36	
Pair 5	TCK1	1.41	0.33	0.00
	TCK2	1.61	0.35	
Pair 6	TPK1	1.74	0.32	0.00
	TPK2	1.60	0.38	
Pair 7	TPCK1	1.41	0.22	0.00
	TPCK2	1.60	0.28	

1 = pre intervention teachers' knowledge (as observed during microteaching) $N = 39*$
2 = post intervention knowledge (as observed during lesson presentation) $N = 38*$
* = One preservice teacher was able to assess three groups. Thus there were multiple responses

Results presented in Table 21 and 22, shows a significant change in knowledge of TPACK between pre-intervention and post-intervention analysis. This entail that, the intervention activities which were carried out by the preservice teachers, during the study were effective in developing TPACK among preservice teachers. Post intervention survey results showed that preservice teachers were able to integrate technology, pedagogy and content in their teaching (Table 23).

Table 23: *Preservice Teachers' Competency in Specific TPACK Related Areas*

	Mean	Std. Deviation
I can teach a lesson that combine science/math, technology and pedagogy	4.18	0.66
I can use strategies that can combine content, technology and pedagogy	4.18	0.66
I can choose technology to use in my classroom that enhances what I teach	4.32	0.57
I can teach a lesson that appropriately combine TPACK	4.23	0.43
I can provide leadership in helping others on the use of TPACK	3.95	0.72

$N = 22$

Although most of the items had a value above the mean in a 5 points scales, where 1 = *strongly disagree* and 5 = *strongly agree*, it was found from data that, preservice teachers' competency in providing leadership on the use of TPACK had the lowest mean and highest standard deviation. This implies that, despite competency in integrating technology, pedagogy and content, a teacher may have, it's not necessarily that he will be able to lead others in the use of TPACK.

Another analysis was carried out to assess the impact of the intervention on the preservice teachers' ability to integrate technology to support various learning activities to learners of different needs. Results showed that preservice teachers' competencies for integrating technology in different learning process were above the mean, in a 6 points scale where 1= *Never*, 2 = *rarely*, 3 = *less than half the time*, 4 = *about half the time*, 5 = *more than half the time* and 6 = *almost always*, for all technology integration competencies assessed (see Table 24).

Table 24: *Preservice teachers' Ability to Integrate Technology in Learning*

	Mean	Std. Deviation
I can integrate technology to support various students learning styles	5.00	1.00
I can integrate technology to facilitate teaching pupils with disability	4.76	1.24
I can integrate technology to support activities that facilitate higher order thinking	4.79	1.29
I can integrate technology to support creativity	4.79	1.49
I can integrate technology to foster pupils' ability to use technology	4.72	1.25
I can integrate technology to support students in learning complex concepts	4.90	1.18
I can integrate technology to enhance students' interests on science and mathematics	4.90	1.21

N = 26

Despite the high mean values as shown in Table 24, the standard deviations were very high, indicating that there was high variability in the preservice teachers' ability to integrate technology in their teaching. This may further imply that, the interventions were effective to some preservice teachers and ineffective to others.

An analysis of preservice teachers' confidence to integrate technology in teaching; showed that preservice teachers competency was above the mean in a 4 points scale, where 1 = *not confident*, 2 = *somewhat confident*, 3 = *confident* and 4 = *very confident* (see Table 25).

Table 25: *Preservice teachers' Areas of Confidence in Technology Integration*

	Mean	Std. Deviation
Use of technology for communication and networking in your course	3.17	1.49
Use of technology for your own development and learning	3.55	1.43
Use of technology to facilitate teaching specific concepts or skills	2.62	0.98
Use of technology to support various students' learning styles	2.97	0.82
Use of technology to facilitate teaching pupils with disabilities	3.03	0.78
Use of technology to facilitate activities that support higher order thinking	2.90	0.98
Use of technology to support creativity	3.00	0.71
Use of technology to foster pupils' ability to use technology in their learning	3.17	0.81
Use of technology to access web information sources e.g. Eric, Google etc	3.38	0.62

N = 26

From Table 25 it's shown that, preservice teachers' confidence to use technology for communication and networking as well as use of technology for personal development had the highest standard deviations. This may mean that some teachers were still not confident in these technology integration aspects even after the training. But overall, preservice teachers agreed to be confident in using technology to support various students' learning activities.

In addition, when responding to open questions about what they learned from the project and the competency they acquired on working with TPACK framework, preservice teachers had different opinions as shown in Table 26. The table presents TPACK related competency that preservice teachers mentioned to have learned and able to demonstrate by using the knowledge they acquired from the interventions. In this table a matrix of responses has been presented, in which the knowledge gained by students is listed on the sides of the table, where as inside the matrix box, are number of preservice teachers who mention a given competency. The numbers presented in the box represents names of the students as were given to each questionnaire during coding process.

Table 26: *Interaction Matrix for Competency Areas and Number of Responses*

What did you learn from the project?	Constructivist learning approach	How to integrate technology in teaching	The concept of TPACK	Integration of technology, pedagogy and content	Choice of technology in relation to pedagogy and content
Constructivist approach	1, 3	1, 26		24	
How to integrate technology in teaching		1	20	19, 23	14, 15
The concept of TPACK			3	16, 17, 18	
The type of technology that enhance learning		4,6,8,9, 10,12,13	2, 25		22
Integration of technology, pedagogy and content		9		3, 4, 5, 7, 11	
Choice of technology in relation to pedagogy and content				3, 4, 5, 7, 11	14, 15

The matrix table shows that, majority of preservice teachers learned the integration of technology, pedagogy and content. Others showed to have learned more about the types of technology that enhance learning and the way those technologies can be integrated in teaching. As reported by the preservice teachers, the TPACK project was useful in developing their knowledge on different constructivist learning approaches, as majority of them were used to common participatory learning approaches: discussion method, role play, brainstorming etc. They also reported to have learned the concept of TPACK and the approaches for choosing a technology to use in relation to pedagogy and content. Preservice teachers' report on what they learned from the project is evidence that the interventions had impact on the development of preservice teachers' knowledge of integrating technology, pedagogy and content, thus an understanding of technological pedagogical content knowledge (TPACK).

Chapter Six

Summary, Discussion, Conclusions and Recommendation

This chapter presents a summary in section 6.1 and discussion of the main findings in section 6.2. It also presents the conclusions in section 6.3 and some recommendations in section 6.4. The chapter comprises of sections about the effective practices for developing technology, pedagogy and content integration competencies as well as the impacts of the intervention activities carried out during the study in developing TPACK competencies.

6.1 Summary of the Findings

This study was intended to investigate ways through which pre-service science and mathematics teachers can acquire ICT competencies to enable them integrate technology, pedagogy and content in their teaching. Its first objective was to assess the preservice teachers' competencies in ICT and its integration with content and pedagogy. Findings revealed that preservice teachers were less competent in technology use and its integration with content and pedagogy. This incompetency was found to be caused by the limited use of technology in learning and accessibility to technological tools. The college was reported to have limited supply of technological tools, which makes it difficult for preservice teachers to practice the use of technology in their learning. Findings further revealed that preservice teachers had no opportunity to learn technology integration approaches from their instructors. It was reported from interview that college instructors are not integrating technology in the classroom because they are as well incompetent in using technology to facilitate teaching. Thus, the preservice teachers' incompetency in technology integration was partly caused by the way they were taught by their teachers at the college. This led to a limited technological knowledge, technological content knowledge, technological pedagogical knowledge and technological pedagogical content knowledge, among preservice teachers.

An analysis of practices that can enhance preservice science and mathematics teachers' competency in integrating technology with pedagogy and content, revealed that the more preservice teachers were engaged in hands on activities that reflects the real teaching environment, the more they learned about technology integration in teaching. Preservice teachers' participation in the process of designing and presenting a lesson in the classroom in a similar way as the real teaching is done, was found to enhance competency in various aspects of technology integration and develop confidence of using technology in teaching. The design of the lesson by using TPACK framework for example, was found to have a number of challenges to preservice teachers, as they had a lot of questions on what to design, how to design and why design about a given topic ... or technology ... or pedagogy and not the other. These questions helped preservice teachers to engage in an inquiry learning process, which required them to read more about TPACK so that they can be able to answer those questions and design a lesson which is free from criticism. Overall, the use of microteaching, lesson design and peer appraisal had the highest mean values and lowest standard deviations, unlike training session which had high standard deviation on the TPACK competency attribute (refer Table 19). This is implying that, theoretical training alone does not enhance knowledge of integrating technology in teaching; rather the combination of theory and practice (hands on activities) is what matters most.

A further analysis was carried out to assess the impacts of the interventions carried out during the study, on the development of the preservice teachers' TPACK competencies. Results showed that, all activities (microteaching, training, lesson design, lesson presentation and peers' appraisal) had significant impact in the development of TPACK knowledge, skills and insights. A paired sample t-test, showed a significant difference between pre-intervention and post-intervention preservice teachers' knowledge of integrating technology, pedagogy and content. Results from both survey and observation (microteaching), showed a positive change on what preservice teachers were able to do with technology before intervention and after intervention. As outcome of the interventions, preservice teachers' confidence in using technology in different science and mathematics' teaching and learning process was enhanced. The interventions helped preservice teachers to develop an understanding of the types of technology that can support constructivists learning approaches as well as the integration of technological knowledge with pedagogical content knowledge. The adoption of hands on activities in the preservice teachers' training process had considerable impact in the development of preservice teachers' technology integration in teaching and thus TPACK.

6.2 Discussion

The overall focus of the study was on how pre-service science and mathematics teachers can acquire competencies for integrating technology pedagogy and content in their teaching. Findings from the study revealed a limited technological knowledge among preservice teachers also limited knowledge of integrating technology, pedagogy and content, thus poor technological pedagogical content knowledge (TPACK). Although preservice teachers had the basic ICT knowledge, they could not integrate this knowledge with content and pedagogical knowledge. The observed incompetency of preservice teachers in technology and its integration with pedagogy and content is attributed to ill-structure and components of the ICT and methodological courses offered to preservice teachers at the college. It is also attributed to instructors' incompetency in integrating technology in teaching which causes preservice teacher to miss the model (an example of a technology integrated learning), as well as the shortage of technological tools.

Further more, ICT courses offered at the college doesn't provide an opportunity for preservice teachers to experience the integration of technology, pedagogy and content. The college offers courses on methodology for teaching different disciplines (physics, chemistry, mathematics etc) also a course on ICT in science and mathematics education. The two courses are taught separately, there is no opportunity for a learner to experience the combination of ICT, science or mathematics and pedagogy. Absence of the opportunity to experience the integration of technology, pedagogy and content, leads to inability of the preservice teachers to practice the integration in teaching. According to UNESCO (2008b) preservice teachers' learning of technology integration in teaching should take into account the curriculum goals (subject matter), pedagogy and ICT. But, preservice teachers at DUCE miss the opportunity to learn and practice the integration of technology pedagogy and content also they miss the model for their technology integration because even their instructors are not integrating these components in the classroom.

Many studies (cf. Beyerbach et al, 2001; LeBaron et al, 2009) report that the quality of teaching with technology depends significantly on the way teachers were taught with technology. The impact of what they learned from the college depends on the extent to which preservice teachers themselves learn with technology (LeBaron et al, 2009; UNESCO, 2008a). Since preservice teachers had a very limited opportunity to learn with technology and their instructors were not a replica to them in teaching with technology; it was obvious that they could not teach with technology, as it was observed during the microteaching session (refer Table 16). Given the fact that, preservice teachers had limited opportunity to develop their technological competencies, this study introduced different learning activities which were intended at developing preservice teachers' competencies in integrating technology, pedagogy and content and thus developing TPACK.

6.2.1 Developing TPACK among Preservice Teachers: Effective Practices

This study has established that, the process of planning a lesson, presenting to colleagues, getting critiques from colleagues and re-planning again in a cyclic way is effective in enhancing preservice teachers' competency in TPACK. The findings of this study agree with those of Somekh, (2008) who found that preservice teachers' participation in different hands on activities was effective in enhancing their technological use in teaching. Participation in activities that reflect the actual teaching gives an opportunity for preservice teachers to learn how to bring together, their technological pedagogical and content knowledge which they learn in separate courses. According to Polly et al. (2009) teachers' technological skills alone are not resulting in the effective use of technology in teaching in ways that are likely to impact students learning. Effective technology integration occurred when preservice teachers participated in activities that enable them to experience firsthand how technology can be effectively integrated in their teaching.

Microteaching was considered among the practices that can enable preservice teachers to reflect the real teaching in a real situation, thus was adopted in this study as one of the practices for enhancing preservice teachers' confidence and competency of working with technology (cf. Jung, 2005; Kilic, 2010; Peker, 2009). As teachers engaged in the process of planning and presenting a lesson to colleagues, they experienced and reflected the challenges and opportunity of teaching with technology in a real field. From the findings, it was found that preservice teachers were unaware of TPACK framework, thus a theoretical training about TPACK framework was important in developing an understanding of technology integration with pedagogy and content. However, the training had no great impact on the development of technological integration knowledge; rather the combination of training and other hands on activities is what made a significant change in the technological pedagogical content knowledge of the preservice teachers. Similarly Flick & Bell (2000) argue that, theoretical understanding of technology is not sufficient to foster effective technology integration in teaching. Instead, technology is supposed to be introduced in the context of science and mathematics teacher education.

Discussions with peers (peers appraisal) which followed after the training and microteaching exposed preservice teachers to several challenges over their presentation and ways in which they can improve their technology integration process. The discussion made preservice teachers to share different views of technology and its integration in teaching (cf. Flick & Bell, 2000). It's the peer appraisal which exposed preserviece teachers to a critical analysis of what they presented in the microteaching in relation to what they learned about TPACK, and what they think could be the best technology integration approach. The discussion about science and mathematics, the teaching approach and technology used during the microteaching, made them to learn more about technology, pedagogy and content and the manner in which they interact (cf. Doering, Hughes & Huffman, 2003).

This study is not the first to realize the importance of integrating activity based learning to develop TPACK competency among preservice teachers. Guzey & Roehrig (2009), Killic (2010) and Niess et al (2009) reported the potentials of hands on activities such as lesson design (what to teach, how to teach and with what technology to teach) in enhancing preservice teachers knowledge of technology, pedagogy and science or mathematics, and thus, TPACK. During the intervention process; it was found that lesson design, had special contribution to the development of technological integration competencies. The lesson design activity subjected preservice teachers in an inquiry thinking process which gave them the opportunity to reflect on the critical relationships between content, technology and pedagogy (cf. Guzey & Roehrig, 2009; Ozgun-Koca et al, 2009). According to Özgün-Koca et al. (2010), as teachers decide whether and how to use technology in their teaching, they need to think critically about the science or mathematics content that they will teach, the technology that they will use, and the pedagogical methods that they will employ. The lesson design was found to be the core for developing technological pedagogical content knowledge among pre-service science and mathematics teachers at DUCE. Lesson design is what determined the quality of presentation and discussion with peers. It was in lesson design where preservice teachers were able to think of the context and the availability of technology in relation to what a teacher was designing.

Good design of a lesson, made the second presentation to be far better than the first one. In the second presentation, one could easily see the integration between technology, pedagogy and content. However, the presentations from mathematics groups were not as nice as those from physics and biology groups. These groups, either failed to get the appropriate program for delivering a given mathematics content, or missed the appropriate pedagogical approach to support learning with technology. Based on this findings, this study agree with Somekh (2008) that computers are not a good fit in mathematics learning if are not supported by other technological tools or mathematics software. Students learning in mathematics require some programs such as drill and practices programs, spreadsheets and software that can provide mathematics formulas and calculations. These facilities missed at DUCE thus making the mathematics presentation uninteresting and ranked low during presentation (see Table 17).

In summary, microteaching acted as a starter to inspire preservice teachers with the thinking of what they learned at the college about technology integration; where as the training acted as a top up to the technological knowledge they already have and peer appraisal acted as a catalyst for redesigning of a lesson that will be free from critics. It was from discussion when presservice teachers showed a new motivation and interest to design a better lesson than what they designed and presented in microteaching. Overall, the opportunity to share knowledge, ideas and challenges with peers was one of the important components of the intervention activities employed in this study. Preservice teachers had an opportunity to reflect back their design and their presentation for future improvement. In general the study adopted the design, implement, evaluate and redesign approach which is widely used in the design based research (McKenney, Nieveen, & van den Akker, 2006). Groups which did not manage to present a lesson which appropriately integrate technology, pedagogy and content were supposed to repeat the lesson, but due to time factor it was not possible to redesign again.

6.2.2 The Impact of Interventions

At the beginning of the lesson (pre-intervention), preservice teachers had no idea of technological pedagogical content knowledge (TPACK). Preservice teachers were also not aware of different technological tools and software that can support learning. Their knowledge about technology integration in learning was limited to PowerPoint use in presentation. After the intervention, preservice teachers' were able to explain the relationship between technology, pedagogy and content in their teaching. During the reflection over the intervention activities, preservice teachers reported to have learned different pedagogical use of ICT, example integrating technology to facilitate different learning styles, to facilitate learning for students with disabilities and facilitate activities that enhance students' higher order thinking. They also reported that, the lesson design process and discussion with peers enhanced their ability to integrate technology to support students in learning complex concepts and enhancing students' creativities. Overall the intervention activities had an impact to the two main stakeholders; the preservice teachers and the college instructors.

Impact to college instructors

Participation of the instructors in the study, gave them an opportunity to assess their own competencies in technology use and the challenges ahead of them in developing technology integration competencies. In realizing that they were incompetent on TPACK, college instructors showed a willingness to discuss in the staff meeting about the instructors' professional development programs to develop technology integration competencies. Studies by Borko (2004), Ferrini-Mundy & Breaux (2008) and Fullan (2003) have prove that in the absence of professional development on instructional technology and curriculum materials that integrate technology use into the lesson content, teachers are not particularly likely to embed technology-based or technology-rich activities into their courses. Thus the decision hereby proposed by the college instructors as strategies to develop their technology integration competencies can be of great importance in having technology integrated by instructors at the college. Development of an understanding of TPACK among college instructors will have an influence over the preservice teachers learning with technology at the college. This will in turn lead to review of ICT and teaching methods courses, so as to address an integrated knowledge of technology, pedagogy and content rather than knowledge of individual aspect of TPACK. The integrated knowledge of technology pedagogy and content would be useful in thinking about what knowledge preservice teachers must have to integrate technology into their teaching and how they might develop this knowledge (Schmidt et al, 2009). This will have a potentially impact on the type of training and professional development experiences that instructors design for both pre-service and in-service teachers.

Impact to Preservice Teachers

The intervention activities were of substantial importance in enhancing preservice teachers' knowledge, ability and skills for integration of technology, pedagogy and content. They also had an opportunity to experience teaching in a way similar to the real situation, thus gaining confidence in working with technology (refer Table 25). Teachers' lack of confidence is reported as one of the reasons for less integration of technology in teaching (Cox et al, 1999; Kirschner et al, 2008). This was worked out during the intervention, whereby after intervention, preservice teachers reported to have confidence in using technology for individual development and learning, for accessing web information and for supporting students' creativity. Preservice teachers' confidence in the use of technology, entails increased probability for them to integrate technology in science and mathematics teaching. Several studies (Cox et al, 1999; Tondeur, Valcke & Braak, 2008; Thomas & Knezek, 2008; Webb, 2008) have reported that, the extent to which technology will be used in teaching depends significantly on the extent to which a teacher is competent and confidence to use technology. An increased understanding of technology and its use in teaching among preservice teachers aids to the development of technological pedagogical content knowledge.

Preservice teachers also reported to have learned the different types of technological tools that can support teaching through different learning activities. Prior to the intervention (TPACK training) preservice teachers' understanding of technology was limited to computer. After the interventions, preservice teachers realized the multitude of technological tools that can support learning in science and mathematics. This, in turn had an effect in the understanding of the selection of technological tools in relation to content and pedagogy as well as the integration of technology pedagogy and content. The difference in pre-intervention and post-intervention TPACK survey and microteaching was evidence of the change in knowledge of preservice teacher on technology pedagogy and content and the manner in which the three components are integrated.

Preservice teachers also claimed to have learned the concept of TPACK and constructivist learning approaches. Pioneers of technology integration in learning (example Collis & Moonen, 2001), advocate the use of constructivist learning approaches; inquiry learning, task based learning, problem based learning, collaborative learning etc. Thus, during the intervention, preservice teachers learned the use of learner centered approaches that are built on constructivist learning approaches. An understanding of constructivist learning approaches, concepts of science and mathematics and the basic knowledge of how technology can support learning, made an integration of technological pedagogical content knowledge possible. This was revealed in the second presentation (lesson presentation) where the interplay between TK, PK, CK, TPK, PCK, TCK and TPACK was clearly seen.

6.3 Conclusion

Findings revealed that preservice teachers at DUCE were competent in content knowledge, pedagogical knowledge and pedagogical content knowledge. Preservice teachers were incompetent in technological knowledge, technological content knowledge, technological pedagogical knowledge and technological pedagogical content knowledge. Paired sample t-test of the impact of the interventions revealed significant change in all TPACK components in which preservice teachers were incompetent. This shows that the interventions were effective in enhancing preservice teaches knowledge of technology integration in teaching which makes up TPACK. It is therefore concluded in this study that, planned interventions that involves preservice teachers in hands on activities have the potentials in developing preservice teachers' competencies in TPACK. The adoption of collaborative approaches which give an opportunity for preservice teachers to solve a problem in groups can have greater impact in the learning of technology, pedagogy and content and the manner they can be integrated in teaching. During the intervention Preservice teachers worked in groups in microteaching, lesson design, presentation and discussion (peers appraisal). Peers groups were found to have substantial impact on all stages of learning about TPACK. This suggests that an adoption of professional learning communities or teacher design teams in developing TPACK competencies among science and mathematics teachers would have greater impacts (cf. Handelzalts, 2009; Hargreaves, 2003; Nieveen, et al, 2005). However, no test was made to find out if there was going to be different results when they work individually. But in their reflection about the interventions, preservice teachers acknowledged collaboration with peers (especially peer appraisal) as an important component of the intervention that made them to understand more about TPACK.

Despite the advantages of collaboration that was demonstrated by the preservice teachers during intervention, their efforts to develop ICT integration competencies were radically retarded by the lack of technological tools. This made some of the preservice teachers to have a limited opportunity to practice the advantages of technology in teaching. As it was noted earlier by Knezek et al (2003), technological tools are one of the important components in enhancing teaching with technology. Thus, for the education to reap the advantage of technology integration process, it is important to ensure sufficient supply of technological tools in addition to technological pedagogical content knowledge. The insufficient supply of technological tools was also found to affect the development of technological knowledge; many of the preservice teachers were not able to practice the use of different technological services such as the use of internet for their own academic development and learning. Preservice teachers are still unaware of the different software and learning support tools available online. The findings of this study revealed that the more preservice teachers were using technology in their learning, the more they gained technological competencies. It is finally hypothesized that, if there were sufficient technological tools in which preservice teachers can access different materials about TPACK, practice the integration of technology pedagogy and content and watch video online that shows how technology is used in teaching, there is likelihood that they would demonstrate better outcomes of intervention than what they presented.

6.4 Recommendations

Given the findings of this study, it is hereby recommended that, technology integration efforts that leads to the development of TPACK, should take into consideration the manner in which science and mathematics teachers can acquire the ICT integration knowledge. The adoption of professional learning communities in which teachers collaboratively design lessons that integrate technology, teach the lesson to colleagues before teaching students and get critiques from colleagues, would be a reliable approach towards successful teachers' development of TPACK.

From this study, it was found that, although preservice teachers were attending courses about ICT in science and mathematics education at the college, they were not competent in integrating ICT with science or mathematics subject for a given pedagogical approach. It is thus recommended that another study should be carried out to redesign the present science and mathematics methodological courses (biology physics chemistry and mathematics teaching methods courses) to integrate technology. At present, these courses pays attention only in content and pedagogy, thus redesigning them to include technology would help in producing preservice teachers who are good in TPACK.

Also, technology integration efforts should not underrate the importance of the availability and accessibility of technological tools to teachers. Teachers' motivation to integrate technology with pedagogy and content can be enhanced by the presence of different learning support technologies such as; iPod, Camera, Wikipedia, Online games, Blogs, Television, Computer, MP3, e-portfolios, discussion forums, CMS and mobile phones etc. Thus, teachers preparation programs should focus not only in developing an understanding of TPACK, but also the manner in which preservice teachers can practice the integration of technology, pedagogy and content. However, the development of TK, PK and CK and the interplay between PCK, TCK and TPK to form TPACK requires availability of technological tools and teachers motivation to integrate the three components. Therefore, the adoption of the will skill and tool model (WST model) for technology integration in teaching (Knezek et al, 2003) is considered important at this place. The two models, TPACK and WST appear to be dependent to each other. Thus a research can be conducted to establish the relationship between the two models and integrate them to form one technology integration model that integrate technological knowledge, content knowledge, pedagogical knowledge, technological tools and teachers willingness. This requires a shift from assessing what preservice teachers learn from the college, to assessing how teachers can effectively implement the knowledge they got from the college in the actual science and mathematics teaching. This will in turn foster the understanding of the relationship existing between TPACK and WST model.

Finally, this study used a small sample of preservice teachers and instructors from one institution, to investigate how preservice teachers can develop technology pedagogy and content knowledge. Also the study used only interview, observation and questionnaires as research instruments, for collecting data during microteaching, lesson design, presentation and peer appraisal. Another study which will have a sample of more students and teachers is important. There is a need for a study that will involve more than one school to build a clear picture of what hinders and what promotes technology integration in science and mathematics teaching. This will provide a better opportunity for establishing a relationship between TPACK and technological skills, TPACK and technological tools and TPACK and teachers' willingness to use technology. The upcoming study is supposed to include the science teachers, school administrators, ICT support team and science students. This will in addition, help to make a link between what preservice teachers learn from the college and what they practice in teaching.

References

Angeli, C. (2005). Transforming a teacher education method course through technology: Effects on preservice teachers' technology competency. *Computers & Education, 45,* 383–398. doi:10.1016/j.compedu.2004.06.002

Beyerbach, B., Walsh, C., & Vannatta, R. (2001). From teaching technology to using technology to enhance student learning: Preservice teachers' changing perceptions of technology infusion. *Journal of Teaching and Teacher Education, 9* (1), 105-127

Beauchamp, G., & Parkinson, J. (2008). Pupils' attitudes towards school science as they transfer from an ict-rich primary school to a secondary school with fewer ict resources: Does ICT matter? *Education Information Technology, 13,* 103-118. DOI 10.1007/s10639-007-9053-5

Borko, H. (2004). *Professional development and teacher learning: Mapping the terrain.* Boulder: University of Colorado.

Collis, B., & Moonen, J. (2001), second printing 2002). *Flexible learning in a digital world: Experiences and expectations.* London: Kogan Page.

Cox, M., Preston, C. & Cox, K. (1999, September). *What motivates teachers to use ict?* Paper presented at the British Educational Research Association Annual Conference. London, UK.

Doering, A., Hughes, J., & Huffman, D. (2003). Preservice teachers: Are we thinking with Technology? *Journal of Research on Technology in Education, 35*(3), 342-363

Dominique, A. M. X & Fereirra, F. (2008). *Perspectives on distance education: open schooling in the 21st century.* British Columbia: Commonwealth of Learning.

Ezeife, A. N. (2003). Using the environment in mathematics and science teaching: an African and aboriginal perspective. *International Review of Education, 49* (3–4), 319–342

Ferrini-Mundy, J., & Breaux, G. A. (2008). Perspectives on research, policy, and the use of technology in mathematics teaching and learning in the United States. In G. W. Blume & M. K. Heid (Eds.), *Research on technology and the teaching and learning of mathematics: Volume 2. Cases and perspectives* (pp. 427-448). Charlotte, NC: Information Age Publishing.

Flick, L., & Bell, R. (2000). Preparing tomorrow's science teachers to use technology: guidelines for science educators. *Contemporary issues in Technology and Teacher Education, 1*(1), 39-60.

Fullan, M. (2003). *Change forces with a vengeance.* London: RoutledgeFalmer

Groth, R., Spickler, D., Bergner, J., Bardzell, M. (2009). A qualitative approach to assessing technological pedagogical content knowledge. *Contemporary Issues in Technology and Teacher Education, 9*(4), 392-411.

Gaible, E., & Burns, M. (2005). *Using technology to train teachers: Appropriate uses of ict in teacher professional development in developing countries.* Washngton DC: infoDev/World Bank

Grundy, S., & Kemmis, S. (1982). Educational action research in Australia: The state o the art (an overview). In S. Kemmis (Ed.), *The action research reader* (p. 83-97). Australia: Deakin University.

Guzey, S. S., & Roehrig, G. H. (2009). Teaching science with technology: Case studies of science teachers' development of technology, pedagogy, and content knowledge. *Contemporary Issues in Technology and Teacher Education, 9*(1), 25-45.

Handelzalts, A. (2009). *Collaborative curriculum development in teacher design team*. Enschede: PrintPartners Ipskamp.

Hare H. (2007). Survey of ICT in Education in Tanzania. In G. Farrell, S. Isaacs & M. Trucano, (eds). *Survey of ict and education in Africa (volume 2): 53 country reports*. Washington, DC: *info*Dev / World Bank

Hargreaves, A. (2003). *Teaching in the knowledge society: education in the age of insecurity*. Berkshire: Open University Press

Harris, J., & Hofer, M. (2009). Instructional planning activity types as vehicles for curriculum-based TPACK development. In C. D. Maddux, (Ed.). *Research highlights in technology and teacher education 2009* (pp. 99-108). Chesapeake, VA: Society for Information Technology in Teacher Education (SITE).

Howden, B. J. (1998). Using action research to enhance the teaching of writing. *Queensland Journal of Educational Research, 14*(1), 45-58.

International Society for Technology in Education (ISTE) (2008). *National educational technology standards for teachers and performance indicators for teachers*. Retrieved 9th February 2010 from http://www.iste.org/Content/NavigationMenu/NETS/ForTeachers/2008Standards/NETS_T_Standards _Final.pdf

International Institute for Communication Development (2010). *Supported programme: ICT-connect-ted – Tanzania*. Retrieved 26th June, 2010 from http://www.iicd.org/supported-projects/tanzania-ict-connect-ted/?searchterm=None

Jimoyiannis, A. (2010). Designing and implementing an integrated technological pedagogical science knowledge framework for science teachers' professional development. *Computers & Education, xxx,* 1–11 doi:10.1016/j.compedu.2010.05.022

Jung, I. (2005). ICT-pedagogy integration in teacher training: application cases worldwide. *Educational Technology & Society, 8*(2), 94-101

Kafanabo, E. J. (2006). *An investigation into interaction between multiple intelligences and performance of learners' in open-ended digital learning tasks*. Pretoria: University of Pretoria.

Keong, C., Horani, S., & Daniel, J. (2005). A study on the use of ICT in mathematics teaching. *Malaysian Online Journal of Instructional Technology, 2*(3), 43-51.

Kilic, A. (2010). Learner-centered microteaching in teacher education. *International Journal of Instruction, 3*(1), 77-100

Kitta, S. (2004*). Enhancing mathematics teachers' pedagogical content knowledge and skills in Tanzania*. Enschede, PrintPartners Ipskamp.

Kirscher, P., Wubbrls, T., & Brekelmans, M. (2008). Benchmarks for teacher education programs in the pedagogical use of ICT. In J. Voogt & G. Knezek. (Eds), *International handbook of information and technology in primary and secondary education*. New York: Springer.

Knezek, G., Christensen, R., & Fluke, R. (2003, April). *Testing a Will, Skill, Tool Model of technology integration*. Paper Presented at the Annual Meeting of the American Educational Research Association. Chicago, IL.

Koehler, M., & Mishra, P. (2009). What is technological pedagogical content knowledge? *Contemporary Issues in Technology and Teacher Education, 9*(1), 60-70

Komba, W., & Nkumbi, E. (2008). Teacher professional development in Tanzania: Perceptions and practices. *Journal of International Cooperation in Education, 11*(3), 67-83

LeBaron, J. & McDonough, E., & Robinson, J. M. (2009). *Research Report for GeSCI Meta-Review of ICT in Education*. Retrieved 13th February, 2010 from http://www.gesci.org/assets/files/Research/meta-research-phase1-F.pdf

Luis, J., Illera, R., & Escofet, A. (2009). A learner-centered approach with the student as the producer of digital materials for hybrid courses. *International Journal of Education and Development using ICT, 5*(1), 23-44

Lundeberg, M., Bergland, M., Klyczek, K., & Hoffman, D. (2003). Using action research to develop preservice teachers' confidence, knowledge and beliefs about technology. *The Journal of Interactive Online Learning. 1* (4), 1-16

Luppicini, R. (2005). A Systems definition of educational technology in society. *Educational Technology & Society, 8* (3), 103-109

Mambo, H.L. (2001). Tanzania: An overview of information communications technology (ict) development in libraries and information services. *Intl. Inform. & Libr. Rev. 33,* 89-96

Marcinkiewicz, H. R. (1993). Computers and teachers: Factors influencing computer use in the classroom. *Journal of Research on Computing in Education, 26*(2), 220-37

Martin, M. O., Mullis I.S., Foy, P., Olson F., Preuscho_E. C., & Alka, E. & Galia, J. (2008). *TIMSS 2007 international mathematics report: Findings from IEA's trends in international mathematics and science study at the fourth and eighth grades*. Boston: TIMSS & PIRLS International Study Center.

Mavroulidou, M., Hughes, S.J., & Hellawell, E.E. (2004). A qualitative tool combining an interaction matrix and a GIS to map vulnerability to traffic induced air pollution. *Journal of Environmental Management, 70,* 283–289

Mcdougall, A. (2008). Models and practices in teacher education programs for teaching with and about it. In J. Voogt, G. Knezek (eds.) *International handbook of information technology in primary and secondary education*. New York: Springer.

McKenney, S. (2001). *Computer-based support for science education materials development in Africa*. Enschede: University of Twente

McKenney, S., Nieveen, N., & van den Akker, J. (2006). Design research from a curriculum perspective. In J. v an den Akker, J., K. Gravemeijer, S. McKenney &, N. Nieveen, *Educational design research* (pp 67-90). London: Routledge.

Mertler, C.A (2006). *Action research: teachers as researcher in the classroom*. Califonia: Sage Publications Inc

Miles, M. B., & Huberman, A.M. (1994). *Qualitative data analysis*. London, SAGE Publication

Mishra, P., & Koehler, M. (2006). Technological Pedagogical Content Knowledge: A Framework for Teacher Knowledge. *Teachers College Record, 108*(6), 1017–1054

Moonen, J. (2008). Evolution of IT and related educational policies in international organisations. In J. Voogt & G. Knezek (Eds.), *International handbook of information technology in primary and secondary education* (pp. 1071-1082). Berlin: Springer Verlag

Mwinsheikke, H. (2003). *Overcoming the language barrier: An in-depth study of the tanzania secondary school science teachers' initiatives in coping with the english-kiswahili dilemma in the teaching-learning process*. Doctoral Thesis, Oslo: University of Oslo

Niess, M.L. (2005). Preparing teachers to teach science and mathematics with technology: Developing a technology pedagogical content knowledge. *Teaching and Teacher Education, 21*, 509–523

Niess, M. L., Ronau, R. N., Shafer, K. G., Driskell, S. O., Harper S. R., Johnston, C., Browning, C., Özgün-Koca, S. A., & Kersaint, G. (2009). Mathematics teacher TPACK standards and development model. *Contemporary Issues in Technology and Teacher Education, 9*(1), 4-24.

Nieveen, N., Handelzalts, A., Akker, J., & Homminga, S. (2005). *Teacher design teams: A scenario for school-based curriculum innovation*. Paper Presented at the ECER, Dublin.

OECD (2009). *CERI – ICT and initial teachers training*. Retrieved on 23rd March 2010 from http://www.oecd.org/document/13/0,3343,en_2649_35845581_41676365_1_1_1_1,00.html

Ottevanger, W., van den Akker, J., & de Feiter, L. (2007). *Developing science, mathematics, and ICT education in Sub-Saharan Africa: Patterns and promising practices*. World Bank Working Paper No.101. Washington D.C: The World Bank.

O-saki K. M. (2007). Science and Mathematics Teacher Preparation in Tanzania: Lessons from Teacher Improvement Projects in Tanzania: 1965-2006. *NUE Journal of International Educational Cooperation, 2*, 51-64.

Özgün-Koca, S. A., Meagher, M., & Edwards, M.T. (2010). Preservice Teachers' Emerging TPACK in a Technology-Rich Methods Class. *The Mathematics Educator, 19*(2), 10–20

Peker, M. (2009). The Use of Expanded microteaching for reducing preservice teachers' teaching anxiety about mathematics. *Scientific Research and Essay, 4*(9), 872-880

Pelgrum, W. (2001). Obstacles to the integration of ICT in education: Results from a worldwide educational assessment. *Computers and Education, 37*, 163–178

Polly, D., Mims, C., Shepherd, C.E., & Inan, F. (2009). Evidence of impact: Transforming teacher education with preparing tomorrow's teachers to teach with technology (PT3) grants. *Teaching and Teacher Education,* xxx, 1-8. Doi. 10.1016/j.tate.2009.10.024

Resta, P., & Laferrière, T. (2008). Issues and challenges related to digital equity. In J. Voogt, G. Knezek (eds.) *International handbook of information technology in primary and secondary education.* New York: Springer.

Schmidt, D., Baran, E., Thompson, A., Koehler, M.J., Mishra, P., & Shin, T. (2009, March). *Examining preservice teachers' development of technological pedagogical content knowledge in an introductory instructional technology course.* Paper presented at the 2009 International Conference of the Society for the Information and Technology & Teacher Education. Charleston: South Carolina.

Senzige, J.P and Sarukesi K. (2003, March). An approach to ICT based school education in Tanzania. *African Studies Association of Australasia and the Pacific 2003 Conference Proceedings - African on a Global Stage 1, Adelaide: Australia*

Shulman, L. S. (1986). Those who understand: Knowledge growth in teaching. *Educational Researcher, 15*(2), 4-14.

Snoeyink, R., & Ertmer, P. (2001). Thrust into technology: how veteran teachers respond. *Journal of Educational Technology Systems, 30* (1), 85–111

Somekh, B. (2008) Factors affecting teachers' pedagogical adoption of ICT. In J. Voogt, G. Knezek (eds.) *International handbook of information technology in primary and secondary education, 449–460.* New York: Springer

Sugiyama, M. (2005*). Exploring the Practical use of ICT tools by Teachers for Making Supplemental Teaching/Learning Materials in Secondary Schools in Tanzania, as an Effort of Supporting Students Learning in Science and Mathematics.* Unpublished, Master's Dissertation. Enschede: University of Twente.

Thomas, L. G., & Knezek, D. G. (2008). Information, communications, and educational technology standards for students, teachers, and school leaders. In J. Voogt, and G. Knezek (eds.) *International handbook of information technology in primary and secondary education.* New York: Springer

Tilya, F. (2003). *Teacher support for the use of MBL in activity-based physics teaching in Tanzania.* Doctoral dissertation. Enschede: University of Twente.

Tilya, F. (2008). IT and educational policy in the sub-saharan african region. In J.Voogt, G. Knezek (eds.) International handbook of information technology in primary and secondary education, 1145–1159.

Tondeur, J., Valcke, M., & Braak, J. (2008). A multidimensional approach to determinants of computer use in primary education: Teacher and school characteristics. *Journal of Computer Assisted Learning, 24, 494-506.*

UNESCO. (2008a). *ICT competency standards for teachers: Implementation guidelines. Version 1.0.* de Fontenoy: UNESCO.

UNESCO. (2008b). *ICT competency standards for teachers: Competency standard modules.* de Fontenoy: UNESCO.

Unwin, T. (2005). Towards a framework for the use of ICT in teacher training in Africa. *Open Learning,* 20(2), 113–129

United Republic of Tanzania [URT], 2003). *National Information and Communication Technology policy.* Dar es salaam: Mture Press

URT (2007). *Information and Communication Technology policy for basic education.* Dar es salaam: Mture Press.

URT (2008). *The education development in the United Republic of Tanzania.* National Report, Ministry of Education and Vocational Training.

URT. (2009). *A framework for ict use in teacher professional development in Tanzania.* Dar es Salaam. Retrieved 22nd February, 2010. from: www.gesci.org/old/files/docman/ICT_TPD_final_Dec_2_09.doc

VanFossen, P. (1999, November). Teachers would have to be crazy not to use the Internet: Secondary social studies teachers in indiana. *Paper Presented at the Annual Meeting of the National Council for the Social Studies,* Orlando: FL

Vesisenaho, M (2007). *Developing university-level introductory ict education in tanzania: acontextualized approach.* Unpublished, Academic Dissertation. Joesnsuu: University of Joensuu

Voogt, J. (1993). Courseware for an inquiry-based science curriculum. An implementation perspective. Enschede: University of Twente.

Voogt, J. (2003). Consequences of ICT for aims, contents, processes, and environments of learning. In J. van den Akker, W. Kuiper & U. Hameyer, (Eds.) *Curriculum landscapes and trends* (pp. 217-236). Dordrecht: Kluwer Academic Publishers

Voogt, J., Tilya, F., & van den Akker, J. (2009). Science teacher learning for MBL-supported student-centered science education in the context of secondary education in Tanzania. *Journal of Science and education and technology, 18,* 429-428. Doi 10.1007/s10956-009-9160-8

Webb, M. (2008). Impact of IT on science education. In J. Voogt, G. Knezek (eds.) *International handbook of information technology in primary and secondary education.* New York: Springer.

Yuen, A., & Ma, W. (2002). Gender differences in teacher computer acceptance. *Journal of Technology and Teacher Education, 10*(3), 123-149

Yunus, A. S & Ali, W. Z. (2009). Motivation in the learning of mathematics. *European Journal of Social Sciences, 7*(4), 93-102

Appendix A: Students' questionnaire

This questionnaire is prepared to collect information concerning student-teachers competency in ICT use, ICT integration in teaching and knowledge on TPACK. The information provided in this questionnaire will be used for reference only. All information will be treated with high confidentiality.

A. Personal information

1. Program of study...
2. Gender...................
3. Your age.........................
4. Do you have teaching experiences? Yes/No..........
   a. If yes, for how long? ....
5. What school subjects are you trained to teach? *Circle all subjects you will teach*
   a. Mathematics
   b. Physics
   c. Chemistry
   d. Biology
6. What educational level do you expect to teach after graduation?
   a. Primary school
   b. Secondary school (O-level)
   c. Secondary school (A-level)
   d. Teachers' college

B. Technology

7. Do you have a computer at home? Yes/No ....
8. Do you have access to internet? Yes/No ....
9. How often do you use computers? .... per day/week/month

In the following questions, check (√) against the appropriate box in accordance to the level of technology use or your competency level

10. What technological devices have you used in the courses you have taken at the college?	Never	Rarely	Less than half the time	About half the time	More than half the time	Almost always
Personal computers (PC)						
Learning management system (Web quest Moodle, ARISI etc)						
Audio equipment						
Digital photo cameras						
Mobile phones						
Projection systems						
Television						
Others (please specify below)						

11. What kind of technological equipment is freely accessible to you as a preservice teacher at DUCE?	Not available	Restricted access	Free access
Personal Computers (Computer Lab)			
Learning management systems (Moodle, ARISI etc)			
Audio equipments (Mp3, radio, etc)			
Digital photo cameras			
Mobile phones			
Projection systems			
Television			
Other (please specificy below)			

12. What learning resources/tools have you used in your courses at DUCE?	Never	Occassionaly	Sometimess	Oftenly	Always
Wikis					
Weblogs					
Social learning communities (facebook, Elgg, netlog, forums etc)					
Google					
Email					
Chat					
Other (please specify below)					

13. Is there any technological support available for preservice teachers at DUCE? (Yes/No/Don't know)

14. If you answered "Yes" in question 6, how would you rate the quality of support? (Poor/Mediocre/Good/Very good).

15. How can you rate your technological competency	Strongly disagree	disagree	Not sure	Agree	Strongly Agree
I can use technology without problems					
I know how to solve my own technical problems					
I can learn technology easily					
I have the technical skills, I need to use technology					
I have sufficient opportunity to work with different technologies at the college					
I keep up with my important new technology					
I know about a lot of different technology					

16. How can you rate your pedagogical competency	Strongly disagree	disagree	Not sure	Agree	Strongly Agree
I know how to assess students performance in the classroom					
I can adapt my teaching based on what students currently understand or do not understand					
I can adapt my teaching style to different learners					
I can assess student learning in multiple ways					
I can use a wide range of teaching approach in a classroom setting					
I am familiar with common student understanding and misconceptions					
I know how to organize and maintain classroom management					

17. How can you rate your content competency (Refer to your subject (s) of specialization)	Strongly disagree	disagree	Not sure	Agree	Strongly Agree
Mathematics					
I have sufficient knowledge about Mathematics					
I can provide sufficient support to learners on a					

mathematics problem					
I have various strategies of developing my understanding about Mathematics					
I know about a lot of different approaches of solving mathematics problems					
Physics					
I have sufficient knowledge about Physics					
I can provide sufficient support to learners on a Physics problem					
I have various strategies of developing my understanding about Physics					
I know about a lot of different approaches of solving physics problems					
Chemistry					
I have sufficient knowledge about Chemistry					
I can provide sufficient support to learners on a Chemistry problem					
I have various strategies of developing my understanding about Chemistry					
I know about a lot of different approaches of solving Chemistry problems					
Biology					
I have sufficient knowledge about Biology					
I can provide sufficient support to learners on a biology problem					
I have various strategies of developing my understanding about biology					
I know about a lot of different approaches of solving biology problems					

18. How can you rate your Technological pedagogical knowledge (TPK) Technological content knowledge (TCK) pedagogical content knowledge (PCK) and technological, pedagogical and content knowledge (TPACK)?	Strongly disagree	disagree	Not sure	Agree	Strongly Agree
PCK					
I know how to select effective teaching approaches to guide students thinking and learning in science/mathematics					
I can easily select the suitable teaching approach for a given subject topic.					
TCK					
I can choose technology that enhances content for a lesson I teach					
I can choose technologies that enhances students' learning for a lesson					
I know about the technology I can use for students' understanding and doing science/mathematics					
TPK					
My teacher education program has caused me to think more deeply about how technology could influence the teaching approaches I use in my classroom					
I can choose technologies that enhance the teaching approaches for a lesson					

I am thinking critically on how I can use technology in teaching					
I can adapt the use of technology that I am learning to different learning activities					
TPACK					
I can teach a lesson that combine science/mathematics, technology and teaching approaches					
I can use strategies that combine content, technology and teaching approaches that I learned at the college, in my own teaching					
I can choose technology to use in my classroom that enhances what I teach, how I teach and what students can learn					
I can provide leadership in helping others to coordinate the use of content, technology and teaching approaches at my school					

C. Pedagogical use of technology

19. To what extent do you expect to integrate technology ...	Never	Rarely	Less than half the time	About half the time	More than half the time	Almost always
... to facilitate teaching-specific concepts or skills						
... to support various students learning styles and to personalize learning						
... to facilitate teaching pupils with disabilities (cognitive, physical etc)						
... to support activities that facilitate higher order thinking						
... to support creativity						
... to foster pupils' ability to use technology in their learning						
... Support students in learning complex concepts						
... enhance students' interest in science and mathematics						
Other (please specify below)						

20. To what extent has the use of technology described below been present in your teaching practicum (field) placements	Never	Rarely	Less than half the time	About half the time	More than half the time	Almost always
a). Use of technology for communication and or networking (colleagues and students)						
b). Use of technology for your own development and learning						
c). Use of technology as a management tool ...						
... for organizing your work and keep records						
... for preparing lessons						
...for finding digital learning resources						

... for designing and producing your own digital learning resources						
d). Use technology to access web information sources e.g. Google & Eric educational resource etc						
Other (please specify below)						

21. To what extent do you feel confident to integrate technology in the following areas	Not confident	Somewhat confident	Confident	Very confident
a). Use of technology for communication and/or networking				
... with students				
...with parents				
... with school management and educational administration				
b. Use of technology for your own development and learning				
c. Use of technology as a management tool				
... for organizing your work and keep records				
... for preparing lessons				
... for finding digital learning resources				
... for designing and producing your own digital learning environment				
d. Your future integration of technology				
... to facilitate teaching specific concepts or skills				
... to support various students learning styles and to personalize learning				
... to facilitate teaching pupils with disabilities (cognitive, physical etc)				
... to support activities that facilitate higher order thinking				
... to support creativity				
... to foster pupils' ability to use technology in their learning				
Use technology to access web information sources e.g. Google & Eric educational resource etc				
Other (please specify)				

22. In the following questions, underline the answer you feel it fits most

a). How would you rate your instructors' confidence on using technology in teaching?	Low confidence	little confidence	good confidence	very good confidence	
b). How would you rate the importance your instructor place on the relevance of ICT in teaching?	No importance	of some importance	quite great importance	very great importance	
c). From your experience of learning with technology what conclusion can you draw about technology in teaching	Technology has no contribution to learning	Technology has little contribution to learning	Technology has satisfactory contribution to learning	Technology has high contribution to learning	Technology has very high contribution to learning

Thank you for you participation

Appendix B: Interview Questions for DUCE Instructors

1. As teachers' instructor, what do you think are the key things that make a good classroom teacher?
   a. How do you implement those things in your own classroom?
   b. What teaching methods do you use?
   c. What importance do you place on ICT in science/mathematics teaching?
2. What can you say about the availability of ICT/technological tools at the college?
   a. Does the availability and type of technological tools affect your decision to use technology in teaching?
   b. How do you use the available ICT tools in teaching pre-service science/mathematics teachers?
3. What, do you feel are the important ICT competencies for you to properly use technology in the preservice teachers' teaching?
   a. How can you evaluate your own competencies in ICT integration in science/mathematics teaching?
   b. Does this level of ICT integration competency you have, affects your motivation to use ICT in teaching?
   c. How do you engage your learners to learn by using ICT?
4. What do you know about TPACK framework?
   a. How do you integrate TPACK in your teaching?
   b. To what extent do you think your technological integration approach can be a replica to science/mathematics preservice teachers you teach?
5. Do you use TPACK as a guide to your lesson plan?
   a. In what ways do you use TPACK framework?
   b. How can you describe the competency level of your students on TPACK?
   c. What do you consider to be strength and or weaknesses of your students in TPACK?
   d. To what extent do you think your students will be able to use ICT in their teaching after graduation?
6. What is your future plan of enhancing technology integration for your preservice teachers' class?

Appendix C: TPACK observation checklist (microteaching and classroom activities)

Subject matter knowledge	Yes	No
1. Clearly introduced the topic and learning goals		
2. Has sufficient knowledge of science/mathematics,		
3. He/she is confident in science/mathematics concepts		
4. Uses appropriate materials in relation to given science/Mathematics topic being taught		
Technological knowledge		
5. Knowledge on learning support tools such as projection tools for presentation; OHP and LCD		
6. Demonstrate fluency in technology systems and the transfer of the knowledge to new situations.		
7. Skills of using communication tools such as email, chat, forums etc to facilitate learning		
Pedagogical knowledge		
8. Engage students in exploring real-world issues and solving authentic problems using digital tools and resources.		
9. Address the diverse needs of all learners by using learner-centered strategies providing equitable access to appropriate digital tools and resources.		
Technological pedagogical knowledge		
10. Engage students in technology based inquiry learning activities		
11. Use technology to help students to collaborate across multiple contexts		
12. Teach and model the use of appropriate pedagogies and technologies for learning		
Technological Content knowledge		
13. Clear link between technology and the content		
14. Design relevant learning experiences that incorporate digital tools and resources to promote student learning and creativity.		
Pedagogical content knowledge		
15. Possess the ability to understand and integrate teaching approaches that arouse students' creativity		
16. Apply teaching approaches which gives more authority to students in solving science/mathematics problem		
Technological Pedagogical and Content Knowledge		
17. Proper choice of technology in relation to content and pedagogy		
18. Clearly integrate the components of TPACK		
19. Clearly apply TPACK frameworks for development, implementation and reflection of the lesson with colleagues and students		
20. Promote students' reflection using collaborative tools to reveal and clarify students' conceptual understanding, thinking and creativity		

Appendix D: Worksheet for Simple Pendulum

Factors affecting its period of oscillation

Aim: To explore the relationship between T, the period of the pendulum and m, the mass of the pendulum bob.

Procedure

Follow the instructions and record your readings and observations.

1. Keep acceleration due to gravity, g at its default setting.

2. Select a length, L and an angular displacement, θ. Keep them constant.

3. Select a value for m.

4. Click on "Start" button to proceed.

5. When the period of the pendulum appears, stop the animation.

6. Note and record T, the period of the pendulum for the selected m in the table below.

7. Reset the applet and repeat Steps 2 to 7 for other values of m.

8. Ensure that the acceleration due to gravity, g, length of pendulum, L and the angular displacement, θ remains the same for different values of m.

Observation

Mass of pendulum bob (g)	50	100	150	200	250
Period T (s)					

Findings

State your findings about the relationship between the period of the pendulum and mass of the pendulum bob.

_____

_____